BODIES AND BATTLEFIELDS

BODIES AND BATTLEFIELDS

Abortion, War, and the Moral Sentiments of Sacrifice

Tadd Ruetenik

CASCADE *Books* • Eugene, Oregon

BODIES AND BATTLEFIELDS
Abortion, War, and the Moral Sentiments of Sacrifice

Copyright © 2021 Tadd Ruetenik. All rights reserved. Except for brief quotations in critical publications or reviews, no part of this book may be reproduced in any manner without prior written permission from the publisher. Write: Permissions, Wipf and Stock Publishers, 199 W. 8th Ave., Suite 3, Eugene, OR 97401.

Cascade Books
An Imprint of Wipf and Stock Publishers
199 W. 8th Ave., Suite 3
Eugene, OR 97401

www.wipfandstock.com

PAPERBACK ISBN: 978-1-7252-7192-0
HARDCOVER ISBN: 978-1-7252-7193-7
EBOOK ISBN: 978-1-7252-7194-4

Cataloguing-in-Publication data:

Names: Ruetenik, Tadd.

Title: Bodies and battlefields : abortion, war, and the moral sentiments of sacrifice / Tadd Ruetenik.

Description: Eugene, OR: Cascade Books, 2021 | Includes bibliographical references and index.

Identifiers: ISBN 978-1-7252-7192-0 (paperback) | ISBN 978-1-7252-7193-7 (hardcover) | ISBN 978-1-7252-7194-4 (ebook)

Subjects: LCSH: Abortion—Religious aspects—Christianity. | Violence—Religious aspects—Christianity. | War—Philosophical aspects. | Sacrifice—United States.

Classification: BR195.A26 .R45 2021 (paperback) | BR195 (ebook)

10/01/21

CONTENTS

Acknowledgments | vii

1 SACRIFICING FOR LIFE; SACRIFICING FOR DEATH | 1
2 THE VARIETIES OF MORAL SENTIMENT | 12
3 ABORTION: A SACRED BATTLE | 24
4 WAR: A SACRED BATTLE | 44
5 GOD HATES WAR: THE ACCIDENTAL PROPHECY
  OF WESTBORO BAPTIST CHURCH | 62
6 HARD CHOICES: VIOLENCE AND SACRIFICE
  IN TONI MORRISON'S *BELOVED* | 75
7 JOHN BROWN, BRING HIM DOWN | 93

Bibliography | 105
Index | 109

ACKNOWLEDGMENTS

I wish most importantly to acknowledge all of the women who have done far more research on the topic of abortion, and have a greater understanding of the issue than I do. I have learned as much as I could.

The two women who have taught me the most, however, are not scholars. My daughter, Nina, has taught me the value of quiet confidence. My wife, Robin, has taught me the value of louder confidence.

1

SACRIFICING FOR LIFE; SACRIFICING FOR DEATH

In her essay "A Baby is Born," Dorothy Day reflects on a 1941 *New York Times* story in which the figure of $17,485,528,049 was given as a budget estimate for US participation in World War II. For some reason she wonders about the last two digits, noting that $49 is about the cost for a poor person to give birth in an area hospital. Day's own publication, *The Catholic Worker*, printed an article about the birth of a boy to a single mother, which she considered "the most beautiful news, the most tragic news, and indeed more worthy of a place in a headline" than how much war costs.

> And this tiny creature, who little realizes his dignity as a member of the Mystical Body of Christ, lies upstairs from me now as I write, swaddled in a blanket and reposing in a laundry basket. He is rosy and calm and satisfied, a look of infinite peace and complacency upon that tiny countenance. He little knows what is in the world, what horrors beset us on every side.[1]

Day's idyllic description makes him sound like the mythical baby Moses, precariously floating through a dangerous world. What is most remarkable about this passage is how it shows Day viewing the birth of a child in a pessimistic way. Pro-life is often thought of as an optimistic attitude about birth. Day, however, sees the event as filled with danger. The blanket swaddles the baby amidst the threat of war and the big budgets it brings

---

1. Day, *Selected Writings*, 157.

with it. He is protected by a force that sees him as a citizen of a country and not merely as a child of God.

Day's description of a child born during war represents much of the spirit in which this book is written. Day has a greater, more comprehensive understanding of life than do many pro-life advocates. Appeals to the innocence of babies—so common in the rhetoric of pro-lifers—are not only aesthetically offensive to some, but even ethically questionable. By insisting on the innocence of babies they suggest that it is possible for babies to be guilty. Babies are not guilty. They just inherit the guilt of a world that thinks it needs large military budgets.

Day continues her reflection by focusing on the single mother:

> There you have the tragedy of the refugee, there you have the misery of homelessness, the uncertainty as to food and clothing and shelter (and this woman had known hunger). And there, too, you have the pain and agony of the flesh. No soldier with his guts spilled out on the battlefield, lying for hours impaled upon barbed wire, suffers physically more than a woman in childbirth.

Day not only raises up the mother, but just as importantly, she brings down the soldier. The mother is superior to the soldier, Day says, because she sees that the suffering of childbirth "brings forth life. In war . . . there is only death."[2] *Bodies and Battlefields* constitutes an elaboration on Day's point. It will show that, if we value the idea of sacrifice at all, we should acknowledge that a woman's sacrifice is morally superior to a warrior's sacrifice, since soldiers kill while mothers do not.

Day's essay makes us compare two types of sacrificial figures: the warrior and the mother. In addition, she focuses our attention on their bodies. The soldier spills intestines, the mother spills an umbilical cord. This focus on bodies and battlefields also shows up in US artist Barbara Kruger's 1989 silkscreen, which depicts a woman's face partitioned with harshly contrasting colors, captioned with the words "Your body is a battleground." Kruger is saying, of course, that she believes that there is a war on women, that the battles between men are ultimately battles against women's bodies, expressed in antiabortion laws. If that interpretation is correct, then the act of abortion can be considered sacrificial. Women fight for control of their bodies, and the result of this is bodily sacrifice. This bodily sacrifice may be considered as referring to both a fetus and a woman. In my view, too much pro-life rhetoric is focused on a vaguely expressed, and often overly

2. Day, *Selected Writings*, 159.

sentimentalized baby, fetus, or embryo victim. If we are to refer to victims, we do better to refer more comprehensively to *sacrificial bodies*. And accordingly, it is both the women *and* the fetus that are sacrificial bodies. It is relevant that one of these bodies chooses the sacrifice and the other body has a choice imposed upon it, and it is also relevant that one of these is uncontroversially considered a body, while the other is not. But it is evident, at least to me, that these questions engage people in metaphysical disputes that can be interminable, and result in people grouping themselves together into warring factions. Before we get down to fighting over bodies and choices, I think it is better that we consider what got us into this position in the first place. Our choices are conditioned by our moral sentiments, and our moral sentiments are conditioned by our culture. My argument is that we have a culture that hides its violence, in part by making it seem that such choices are inevitable.

In *Bodies and Battlefields* I will look at both the violence of war and the violence of abortion. Immediately, however, we encounter a problem with the use of "violence." Those who tend to defend war cannot deny that war is violent, but they can and do deny that such violence is necessarily bad. Some of those who defend abortion believe that violence is bad but that abortion should not be considered violent. Or, in another approach, abortion rights advocates acknowledge that abortion is violent, but in a tragic or sacrificial sense. This book will assert that both war and abortion are violent and need to end.

In doing so, the moral authority of nonviolence will be assumed. To answer questions about when war or abortion are justified would be to give in to the notorious technique of counterexample that philosophers use, and which creates an excessive focus on exceptional and often horrific cases. When someone says that they are against abortion or war, an opponent activates their violent imagination, devising scenarios such as "What if your wife were being raped?" or "What if you see Americans about to be beheaded?" We are not interested in considering morbid scenarios. There is no reason we must mentally plan for violent acts. If such acts happen, it is not the obligation of the victims to explain how they are going to act. In such scenarios whatever happens happens. The goal should be to persistently oppose violence while working to develop habits that make the violent scenarios more and more ridiculous to consider.

Philosopher Cornel West identifies himself as a prophetic pragmatist, one who is tied to a "tradition of prophets who brought urgent and compassionate critique to bear on the evils of their day."[3] This book takes up that call, but also focuses its prophetic glare at our ideas of compassion themselves. I believe our problem is not necessarily a lack of compassion. The problem is that we have allowed killing to be rationalized as an act of compassion. Compassion can serve as a cover-up for violence. This is the case both with wars done out of concern for oppressed people, and abortions done out of concern for the inordinate burden that women have in all matters of reproduction. We do not necessarily need more compassion; rather, we need to better direct our compassion, and imagine ways of acting compassionately that do not involve killing as a response to social and political problems. Doing so might mean making radical social and political transformations.

At the least, it will require more sophisticated ways of looking at pro-life ethics. For one example, there is the 2010 book *Consistently Pro-Life: The Ethics of Bloodshed in Ancient Christianity*, by theologian Rob Arner. Arner argues against abortion, against war, against capital punishment, and against euthanasia. While I am supportive of the consistently pro-life position, I believe it has limits. The idea of consistency implies a legal and intellectual understanding of morality that is simply too narrow to reflect our habitual and emotional responses to these topics. Although it provides a sense of rational purity that suggests justice, it just does not reflect the emotional and even sentimental nature of our attitudes about matters of life, death, and killing. Saying that someone needs to be consistent in their views implies that morality is a strategy game governed by rules. And these rules are to be followed by all, although used to the advantage of the more cunning. For example, pointing out a contradiction in an opponent's argument is a common technique of both amateur and professional philosophers. But although the contradiction identifier gains a sense of rational superiority, the loser does not necessarily change their mind. When you lose at a game of strategy, you just assume you either had insufficient understanding of how to use the rules, or knew the rules but were temporarily embarrassed by bad luck in the chance elements of the game. You regroup for a rematch, trying to learn from those who defeated you, trying to be more like them in order to defeat them.

If we are to wage a nonviolent war against violence, it will not be done by following the rules of war. If we play by the rules, the warriors of violence, deeply familiar with rules and strategies, will have the advantage. The

---

3. C. West, *Reader*, 171.

war against war needs to be fought as a *guerrilla*; otherwise the advantage goes to the always superior organization of the rational war mind.

THE SACRAMENTS OF ABORTION AND WAR

In popular media, we find a constant conjunction of the terms *pro-life* and *abortion*, but no such conjunction of the terms *pro-life* and *war*. This is not simply a matter of inconsistency. The problem is a lack of appropriate *comprehension*. When we comprehend something, we (noticing the literal sense of the word) grab things and put them together. The goal is to notice and respond to everything. Consistency often requires us to reject something; comprehension requires that we see everything. We have to see both the charred bodies of enemy soldiers and the ripped flesh of fetuses, and try to understand why both of these things happen. We do not have to believe that the flesh of soldiers and the flesh of fetuses have morally equivalent consideration, but we cannot deny that they have important similarities, and more important, we cannot put ourselves in a situation in which one of them is rationalized into moral insignificance.

In a 1992 book titled *The Psychology of Abortion*, social psychologist Ginette Paris says that "we have taken more lives in the name of faith, race, regime, party, or progress, relatively speaking, than the archaic societies sacrificed to their most bloodthirsty gods." She notes that a thousand times more pagans have been massacred by Christians than Christians have been sacrificed by pagans.[4] So considered, she says, Christians are hypocritical to be pro-life. She is correct. However, Paris's argument is supplemented with a revealing story regarding her interaction with her daughter, who after having just watched a documentary about war was now watching an interview with a male antiabortion demonstrator.

> My daughter's reaction showed me how surprisingly sensible adolescents can be when they consider the adult world. She could neither understand nor accept that the horrors shown in the documentary were permissible legal actions sanctioned and funded by governments, forgiven and sometimes even blessed by the Church. To be allowed to kill men, women, and children who are full of life and fully conscious of suffering, a simple formula is needed—a declaration of war. These same men who decide whether or not to kill in war then dare to talk about crime and murder when a

---

4. Paris, *Psychology of Abortion*, 36.

woman sacrifices a fetus no bigger than a raisin and less conscious than a chicken.⁵

Paris seems to accept war insofar as it can be used to accuse certain people of hypocrisy. And indeed it is hypocritical that men who choose war are often adamantly against women choosing abortion. But this hypocrisy can be fixed by just taking a consistently pro-killing position. One who accepts killing some beings full of life in addition to those less full of it can be praised only for the small virtue of rational purity. The author notes the "simple formula" of a declaration of war, but a declaration of choice to abort is also a simple formula. To follow this simple formula, Paris denies the significance of what appears to be just a raisin in the womb and allows the aerial bomber to deny the significance of what appear to be just raisins on the Earth.

Paris's opinion about war and abortion is partly correct. The problem is in accepting the terms of war, perhaps taking the male perspective that sees itself as in charge of life and death. It is here that Progressive Era philosopher Jane Addams, who lived through the two World Wars, helps us shift emphasis from violent patriarchy to protective matriarchy. When considering what men say to women in arguing against their fitness for voting, Addams retorts that men "are so fond of fighting—you always have been since you were little boys. You'd very likely forget that the real object of the State is to nurture and protect life." If men did not have the right to vote, Addams considers, the argument would be that by giving them such control, we would be "voting away huge sums of money for battleships" because men are "so ready to lose their heads over mere military display"⁶ and harbor "such curious survivals of the mere savage instinct of punishment and revenge."⁷

Considering Addams's clever reversal, we now see that it is Paris's daughter, more than Paris herself, who has the right sentiments. There was no indication in the story presented that her daughter was anything other than anti-killing. Her sensibilities are perhaps a less dramatic version of those of Natasha Rostov, a character in Leo Tolstoy's *War and Peace*. At her Russian Orthodox church, Rostov prays nobly for peace "without distinction of class, without enmity, united in brotherly love." This moment of exalted peace is jostled by the sudden appearance of a deacon presenting

---

5. Paris, *Psychology of Abortion*, 21.
6. Addams, *Reader*, 108.
7. Addams, *Reader*, 111.

a prayer just received from the Synod. The prayer speaks of protection against "this foe confounding Thy land, desiring to lay waste to the whole world." Russia's protector is Tsar Alexander, whom the prayer exalts as "our most worshipful and supreme Sovereign," whose army has "taken up arms in Thy name" in order to oppose "those who hate us and our Orthodox faith" and who thus should be "put to shame and perish." The narrator then describes how Natasha

> could not pray that her enemies might be crushed underfoot when only a few minutes before she had been wishing she had more of them to love and pray for. Yet neither could she doubt the justness of the prayer that was being read on bended knees. She felt in her heart a devout and tremulous awe at the punishment that overtakes men for their sins, and especially of her own sins, and she prayed God to forgive them all, and her too, and to grant them all peace and happiness. And it seemed to her that God heard her prayer.[8]

Natasha found herself facing two things: the universal Christian requirement to love one's neighbors and the particular wish of the Russians to destroy theirs. Having to consider Christianity along with nationalism places Natasha in a position of self-sacrifice.

Ultimately, Natasha decides against militarism and adopts a position of personal pacifism, reflecting the position of Tolstoy himself. In his *Confession*, Tolstoy says that he too went through a similar uncomfortable conflict of sentiments while trying to attend church: "I interpreted the frequent repetition of prayers for the Tsar and his family by the fact that they are more exposed to temptation than others, and the prayers for the subjugation of our enemies and adversaries by saying that they are evil." As a result, he says, most of the church experience was meaningless to him.[9]

AN END TO CONSISTENCY

Ralph Waldo Emerson's prose poem "Self-Reliance" contains this famous line: "A foolish consistency is the hobgoblin of little minds, adored by little statesmen and philosophers and divines."[10] In this work, we can understand as foolish the kind of consistency that would concern itself with consistent

---

8. Tolstoy, *War and Peace*, 768–69.
9. Tolstoy, *Confession*, 70.
10. Emerson, *Writings*, 138.

killing more than consistent non-killing. Law indeed tends toward consistency, while ethics is larger than law. We are walking cluster concepts, able to tolerate intersections at the outer levels, and only become disturbed whenever we get close enough to each other that our cores get compressed. Walt Whitman, for example, strengthens the Emersonian idea in his famous "Song of Myself":

> Do I contradict myself?
> Very well, then I contradict myself.
> I am large, I contain multitudes.[11]

We need more largeness and less consistency in our world. This will help us avoid hypocrisy. The question becomes "How many things can we not kill?" not "How can we ensure we are killing consistently?" Pro-choice people often criticize pro-life people for only caring about life when it is in the womb, and not caring to provide the positive conditions for life outside of the womb. If it can be said that antiabortion people only care about life in the womb, it can also be said that pro-choice people only care about life outside of the womb. *The answer here is to be expansive in our care. The challenge, however, is not to misinterpret violence as a form of care.*

With abortion—but also with war—the debates often proceed predictably into circling discussions of what counts as life. This idea is often talked about in metaphysical terms, and people invoke science, theology, and whatever else they need to justify their assertion about what life *really* is. A definition of life, however, often works in service of the ethical position one endorses, and not the other way around. So to say, for example, that a fetus has life is to say, ultimately, that you should not kill it. The point, however, should not be that it's important to be careful about what "has" life, but that it's important not to kill.

The arguments in this book might not be able completely to avoid getting involved in the "But what counts as life?" question. It is admittedly difficult to separate the idea of killing from the idea of life. They go together. But instead of focusing on what precisely counts as life, perhaps we can focus on not doing things that are similar to what we think of as killing. So the goal of this book is not to establish a metaphysical classification of objects, but to promote certain ethical practices. Life is the good, the truth, and the beauty to which we aspire; and violence and injustice is the evil we avoid. We call something "living" not in the sense that we call a dress "red,"

---

11. Whitman, "Song of Myself," 43.

for example. We call something living as a way of saying that that thing has a high value, one that approaches infinity. Life is not a quality of a substance but an ethical assertion about a practice. So for those who contend that it begs the question to say we should avoid killing without first establishing the value of that which is to be protected from killing, my guerrilla-warfare response is to invoke Whitman, in paraphrase:

> Do I beg the question?
> Very well, then I beg the question.
> (I am a circle. I am comprehensive.)

So as for the metaphysicians engaged in the "But what counts as life?" battle, we will leave the dead to bury the dead. We are investigating the attitudes of violence and sacrifice. But even when dealing with relatively vague cultural forces, one can be clear about personal motivations. The attitude here is decidedly antiabortion, and even more decidedly anti-war. In these respects we will take the comprehensive view: stopping abortion should be done through addressing the reasons and causes for abortion; stopping war should be done through addressing the reasons and causes for war. We are focused on "thou shalt not kill" both in and out of the womb, and "thou shalt not kill" both in and out of the war zone. Doing so might involve monetary costs far greater than what Dorothy Day or the military-industrial complex can envision. But if we believe life has infinite value, it will be worth it.

THE AUTHOR'S CONFESSION

I have no experience of war, and further I am not a woman, so my understanding is limited on abortion. Nonetheless, I present my own case, one that involved, in part, sexual irresponsibility. When I was eighteen, my nineteen-year-old girlfriend became pregnant. After floating the idea of getting "hitched"—an understandable euphemism directed at a young man who had never seriously thought about the idea—she then responded to my moral catatonia by presenting the option of "getting it taken care of." If I remember correctly, it would cost $200, which was no major impediment for a White suburban kid to procure. The abortion option was a live one to me, and I remember saying—with what seemed to me to be a special maturity about the issue—that that made sense because what we were talking about was "this small," making a gesture with my index and thumb indicating a shrimp-sized object.

I mention a shrimp-sized object because, a week or so after the abortion, my girlfriend and I were eating at a restaurant. The procedure had gone well, and although I panicked a bit just before it began, and was referred along with my girlfriend to an *ad hoc* counselor, I recalled little of what happened. We were now, however, sitting at the table, otherwise enjoying our time together, when I saw the shrimp on the plate in front of me. That to which I had a week earlier indicated with my fingers was now in front of me, and I was ready to consume it. This caused a considerable splash of anxious pain, and although the immediate feelings dissipated, I had longer and more terrifying episodes in the weeks after. The episode contributed to me becoming vegetarian.

Through rationalization I gradually came to a tentative peace about it. But for quite a while afterward the idea of abortion continually triggered the thought, as odd as it sounds, that *I* committed abortion. Peace occurred only when I insisted to myself that it was *she* who made the choice, not I. Even though I likely could have stopped the abortion by making certain promises, it was nonetheless *she* who did it. It was about her; the abortion, ultimately, did not belong to me. I welcomed the idea of being removed from ultimate responsibility, even though it is not clear that I should have. I left her alone. Alone with only choice. A month later, we were no longer a couple. I am not sure why that happened, but presumably I was distracted by other things in my life.

In his essay "The Moral Equivalent of War," philosopher William James meditates on the complex psychology involved with understanding the American Civil War.

> There is something highly paradoxical in the modern man's relation to war. Ask all our millions, north and south, whether they would vote now (were such a thing possible) to have our war for the Union expunged from history, and the record of a peaceful transition to the present time substituted for that of its marches and battles, and probably hardly a handful of eccentrics would say yes. Those ancestors, those efforts, those memories and legends, are the most ideal part of what we now own together, a sacred spiritual possession worth more than all the blood poured out. Yet ask those same people whether they would be willing, in cold blood, to start another civil war now to gain another similar possession, and not one man or woman would vote for the proposition. In modern

eyes, precious though wars may be they must not be waged solely for the sake of the ideal harvest. Only when forced upon one, is a war now thought permissible.[12]

James is saying that we somehow look at the Civil War as a necessary part of our history, although we would never choose to do it again. But we chose it at the time, and James seems to be referring to a kind of bad faith on our part. We hate war, but we do not want to do without it. Or perhaps we start wars knowing that later we can repudiate what we wanted to do at the time. There is something similar in my understanding of the abortion, and it disturbs me. It is the bad faith of feeling and believing that something is forced, but feeling and knowing that it was free.

Just as disturbing is what my girlfriend said later to me, namely that she believed having an abortion could somehow bring us together as a couple. Looking back now, it is not that I think she was mistaken; it's that she was right, unfortunately. The loss of the shrimp-sized object, and the almost ritualistic process by which it was lost, did have the potential to bring my girlfriend and I together. Although I did indeed let the relationship fade, it still gives me an uncanny warm feeling, a "sacred spiritual possession" that I have in addition to the lingering guilt, anxiety, and occasional moral panic about what happened. Were we forced into the abortion, the way that James, at the end of the quote, says that we now believe we are forced into war? Almost certainly not. We were middle-class young adults with resources, both economic and social, to take care of a child. There seems, on the contrary, to be a kind of "ideal harvest" involved. The abortion was, it seems, a *chosen* sacrifice.

As for me, I feel that I made a cowardly choice. I could have seen the pregnancy as a noble calling, stayed with the woman, and been the father to a child. Friends of mine did exactly that, and I see myself how a man who avoided wartime military service sees himself in relation to the friends who served.

---

12. James, *Heart*, 13.

2

THE VARIETIES OF MORAL SENTIMENT

The idea of moral sentiment used in this book comes in part from Ralph Waldo Emerson. In his "Divinity School Address," for example, he speaks about his spiritual brethren:

> The divine bards are the friends of my virtue, of my intellect, of my strength. They admonish me, that the gleams which flash across my mind, are not mine, but God's; that they had the like, and were not disobedient to the heavenly vision. So I love them. Noble provocations go out from them, inviting me to resist evil; to subdue the world; and to Be. And thus by his holy thoughts, Jesus serves us, and thus only. To aim to convert a man by miracles, is a profanation of the soul. A true conversion, a true Christ, is now, as always, to be made by the reception of beautiful sentiments.[1]

Emerson asserts that we should follow religious geniuses not because they dazzle us with supernatural influence, but because we believe they have moral sentiments similar to ours. The word *sentiment* probably should not be confused with *sentimental*. The sentimental is surface-level moral sentiment for those who do not go deeper. Sentimentality is to morality what sappiness is to art: a cover-up emotionality resulting from incomplete discernment. The moral sentiment is more like a *sediment*. We might call it a deposit of cultural values in the individual. It is quieter, but more enduring than both personal reflex and cultural habit. It is a clarification of personal

---

1. Emerson, *Writings*, 69.

principles and social values, and we believe along with Emerson that it is possible to share sentiments with others in the same way that all parts of a river share the same bed if they share anything at all.

The moral sentiment is not merely subjective, nor is it an ancestral inheritance that completely determines our fate. The root *sent-* here connects to mind in the expansive sense, before our idea of it became divided, for example, into feeling and reason. Philosopher Ellen Kappy Suckiel notes that Emerson's use of "Reason" is unusual, referring to "a faculty of transcendental intuition," an "instinct" that cuts through the "distinctions, hesitations, and indirectness of discursive thought."[2] The current, specialized use of the term *reason*, referring to abstractions and language technicalities, is a result of our fallen state.

According to Mexican philosopher Jose Vasconcelos, specialized reason is a sign of a culture's lack of spiritual development. In *La Raza Cosmica*, he presents the development of humanity as involving three stages: the material, in which tribes war with each other and establish agreements based on self-interest; the intellectual, in which universal laws dominate human relations; and the spiritual, in which we guide ourselves by true sentiments and transcendent beauty. As he explains:

> En vez de reglas, inspiración constante. Y no se buscará el mérito de una acción en su resultado inmediato y palpable, como ocurre en el primer período; ni tampoco se atenderá a que se adapte a determinadas reglas de razón pura: el mismo imperativo ético será sobrepujado, y más allá del bien y de mal, en el mundo del pathos estético, sólo importará que el acto, por su bello, produzca dicha. Hacer nuestro antojo, no nuestro deber; seguir el sendero del gusto, no el de apetito ni el del silogismo; vivir el júbilo fundado en amor, esa es la tercera etapa.[3]

As Vasconcelos explains it, the spiritual state seems to be a synthesis of the material and the intellectual, not the hot-blooded desire of the warrior or the cold reason of the judge. But neither is it a lukewarm compromise. The

---

2. Suckiel, *Heaven's Champion*, 137

3. Vasconcelos, *La raza cósmica*, 69. "Instead of rules, constant inspiration. The merit of an action will not be sought in the immediate and tangible results, as in the first period; nor will it be required to adapt itself to predetermined rules of pure reason. The ethical imperative itself will be surpassed. Beyond good and evil, in a world of aesthetic *pathos*, the only thing that will matter will be that the act, being beautiful, shall produce joy. To do our whim, not our duty; to follow the path of taste, not of appetite or syllogism; to live joy grounded on love—such is the third stage" (29, English translation).

spiritual stage involves both of the former stages as something more intense than either alone.

The moral sentiment can be understood as a synthesis of subjective and objective, of the ethical and the aesthetic. Although it is based on personal taste, it also can be asserted as universal. Philosopher Immanuel Kant, known for his cold reason, defined beauty as what happens when a person is pleased by something without having a subjective interest in it. Because of this, Kant says, the judgment of beauty is something that should be intended to apply to everyone. When we *really* like something, we do more than personally like it. We imply that all should like it as well. Emerson believes that "the inmost in due time becomes the outmost, and our first thought is rendered back to us by the trumpets of the Last Judgment."[4] As we become increasingly inmost, large becomes the new small. Jesus says the kingdom of God is within, while Emerson believes the same, but with a different emphasis: the kingdom of Man is without.

So when we hear someone tell a story with a cracking voice or eyes wet with tears, or when the presentations of such stories evoke a lump in the throat or welled-up eyes in those listening, we are seeing the inner appreciation of beauty in the outer world of signs and symbols. One does not tell stories just for one's own appreciation. By their nature, stories are for others' consideration, and the tears and trembling voice mean that the individual's sentiment is not just for the individual, but for everyone. Tears come with a demand that others should feel the same way, and this is why when someone is emotional while telling a story, we can feel guilty about not feeling the same. Even if the story is personal, it is still founded upon a sentiment that feels universal.

We cannot assume, however, that a teary presentation is a sufficient sign of moral sentiment. For one, such signs are capable of being faked. Emerson says that in forcing a smile in a boring conversation "the muscles, not spontaneously moved but moved by a low usurping willfulness, grow tight about the outline of the face, with a most disagreeable sensation."[5] Others notice fakery as well. According to philosopher Denis Dutton, humans have developed a sophisticated, instinctive capacity for fraud detection. He says that humans have developed through evolution a "skeptical sensitivity regarding signals "open to any degree of fakery."

---

4. Emerson, *Writings*, 132.
5. Emerson, *Writings*, 137.

THE VARIETIES OF MORAL SENTIMENT

Human abilities to make critical distinctions in responding to evolved cues and signals are effortless and acute. Human critical discrimination in signals requires very little training to get it going: it is spontaneous, often a component of gossip, and even pleasurable—always the mark of an evolved capacity. "That suit's an Armani? I don't believe it." "I can't tell if she dyes her hair, but it's gorgeous." "How can I take seriously a so-called professor who keeps saying 'ek cetera'?"[6]

What follows is a selection of contemporary anecdotes intended to discern true from fake moral sentiment, that is, to find sentiment below sentimentality. The moral sentiment is a mindfulness of universal balance and wholeness that inclines us toward veneration.[7] So considered, discernment of this moral sentiment involves criticism of the big picture rather than just the details, and if we are to assert our own inmost sentiment against another, we do so by showing ours to be more expansive and inclusive, but not so abstract as to divorce mind from the body of sense. It is evolutionarily developed, and thus changeable, but should not be trivialized as just a survival adaptation. The moral sentiment can be prodded by joy and levity, but it is only with seriousness that it can be fully encountered.

The following anecdotes are in some cases particular events and in other cases idealized versions of more general events. They all have been fashioned as an attempt to enunciate sentimentalities and sentiments involving violence expressed in sometimes heavily sublimated ways. They are idiosyncratic choices of the author, but as Emerson believes, to be truly idiosyncratic is to participate in transcendental virtue.

1. *A disc-chasing dog.* It is unlikely I am alone in finding something more than merely entertaining in the phenomenon of a disc-chasing dog. We often find it vicariously thrilling to watch the physical exertion of animals, human or otherwise. This is perhaps due to our own laziness and enjoyment in exploitation, but it feels like such a wholesome experience. As the disc is thrown, the sprinting canine's head seems to morph into a vector of intention. Lips drawn back, eyes bulging, we see the aggressive smile of a predator using its instincts. We become conscious of the act of tracking, bred into the animal through evolution. And the animal is so *into it*, as if its whole being were involved in

---

6. Dutton, *Art Instinct*, 153.
7. Richardson, *Mind on Fire*, 289.

the goal, with nothing else confusing its simple soul. Such pure mind-body intention is the envy of any human athlete.

"Enjoyment" is too shallow of a word here. The animal engages in a religious devotion involving mind, body, and soul. And the event is not just fun; it seems *moral*. If made aware that the dog is just tracking its prey reflexively, we ignore this fact, because the hunt has been transformed into something higher, something nonviolent. We would cringe and grow somber seeing the leap of a jackal succeed in teeth-grabbing a bird's body, but we smile and applaud every time the border collie lands with the disc in its mouth. This athleticism is, I would like to think, just as natural as predation.

Appreciating the full situation involves considering both the disc thrower and the audience. The thrower is the dog's friend. The audience wants to be the dog's friend. All beings at the event are in a conspiracy of joy, wanting to experience the successful throws, leaps, catches, and the ensuing applause. The situation is similar to what Emerson describes "Self-Reliance" when he speaks of youth: "Infancy conforms to nobody: all conform to it, so that one babe commonly makes four or five out of the adults who prattle and play to it."[8] Likewise, one disc-chasing dog creates a crowd of devotees. Jesus said to let the children come to him, because the kingdom of God belongs to them (Matthew 19:14). If he had had a disc, he would have flung it and said let the dogs go to it, and for the same reason.

2. *A funeral for a police dog.* It is remarkable how much a funeral for a police dog can bring out the moral sentiment among humans. People are compelled to believe that this animal understands duty, even though if pressed on the matter, people would generally deny such morality to animals. Duty often refers to doing something for an ideal rather than a personal interest. It is unclear that dogs have similar motivations, though, since apprehending a perpetrator might be as instinctual, if not also as enjoyable, as chasing a disc. To think of it as instinct would rob the police dog funeral of its poignancy, but it would fit in with our other common attitudes toward animals, namely that they lack certain human capacities and thus do not get the same moral consideration as humans.

---

8. Emerson, *Writings*, 134.

Humans' beliefs on this matter remain confused. If we praise a dog for its virtue in chasing a perpetrator, it seems we also should blame the dog if it kills a squirrel, which has done nothing wrong. Since we do not blame the dog, we cannot seriously praise it either, and must look for a different source of the moral sentiment. I suggest that we are not so much approving of dutiful serving, but are responding to the deep and perhaps evolutionarily conditioned sense of *sacrifice* that the dog signifies. We believe that a human officer sacrifices himself for the safety of the community, and we believe the police dog sacrifices himself for the safety of the officer. Officer K9 is thus a sacrifice within a sacrifice.

We cannot process the death of a police dog in the usual ways of considering retributive justice. The suspect who kills a police dog cannot seriously be considered a murderer without one also taking seriously, for example, the idea that most meat-eating humans are complicit in animal murder. The suspect who kills an attacking police dog is arguably *more* justified in doing so, since he is, unlike the meat-eater, being attacked. The suspect is not charged with murder, even if he is charged with something more than destroying property. This discloses, then, that even while being reverential toward the police dog, we still believe in maintaining a moral hierarchy of species.

3. *Spontaneous actions amidst family tragedy.* Religious author Devin Schadt provides the following story, one that is almost too tragic to retell:

> An acquaintance of mine, Jay, was watching his eighteen-month-old son in his backyard. For only a moment, he took his eyes off of him. It was just enough time for the child to leave the yard, while Jay's sixteen-year-old daughter was backing the car out of the driveway. She backed over the little boy. As Jay held the dead body of his son, he had enough wherewithal to embrace his daughter simultaneously. Jay lost a son that day, but he refused to also lose a daughter[9]
>
> Jay never blamed his daughter for his son's death, but instead endured the trial with her. Together they grieved their loss. Jay's love and forgiveness were so tender that his daughter forgave herself, eventually married, had her own child, and in that child, Jay and his daughter rejoiced—and still rejoice. Today, Jay

---

9. Schadt, *Father,* 156–57.

says through tears, "I think that event has taught me how much God the Father loves us and forgives us, despite what we've done to His Son."[10]

When Emerson talked about spontaneous impressions, he was using "spontaneous" in the philosophical sense: experiencing something without mediation. In this story, however, the more ordinary, temporal use of the term is highlighted. The father *immediately* decides to comfort his daughter. Schadt's story brings out how father reaches out to daughter with a love-reflex, even while seeing that she was the proximate cause of the son's death. There was something stronger in the father that overcame the reflex of revenge. People often impulsively react to evil situations with anger, blame, and violence. Later, they might realize that blame is misplaced, dispersed, or even, as is the case here, irrelevant.

The family context needs further consideration. The father's love-reflex was, in a sense, understandable. As Schadt describes it, his intuition involved not losing *his* daughter, along with *his* son. Emerson expresses the Christian condition forcefully when he asks: "Why should we assume the faults of our friend, or wife, or father, or child, because they sit around our hearth, or are said to have the same blood? All men have my blood and I all men's."[11] If the proximate cause of the death had been someone outside of the family, it is unclear whether Jay would have reacted as nobly, but rather have given in to the immediate impulse of revenge. Were this a visiting friend, or a stranger, or someone who was obviously negligent (texting while driving, for example) the man's embrace or instant forgiveness would have been more remarkable and evocative of an even more profound Christian sentiment.

4. *A Danish baby laughing with his father.* After the preceding example of unspeakable tragedy, it is reassuring to read a story about unspeakable and yet ordinary joy. With millions of worldwide views, the 2006 video of a laughing Danish baby[12] is so simple that its fame appears accidental. A child sits in a high chair, laughing to the crisp "bong" sound vocalized by his father every few seconds. Each meaningless

---

10. Schadt, *Father*, 156–57.
11. Emerson, *Writings*, 145.
12. *Laughing Baby*. https://www.youtube.com/watch?v=HttF5HVYtlQ.

sound elicits a contagious peal of laughter from the boy, who stares ahead, waiting for each new irruption of sound. The father begins to break character himself after a while, and chuckles at the whole event. Meanwhile, the viewers are laughing and appreciating an even larger phenomenon: the boy's unconscious laughing, the father's joyful prompts; and the belief that this can be appreciated across all cultures. The meaningless of the sound makes the event more beautiful, the unreflective joy of a child responding to father.

While Emerson's wife Lidian was away for two weeks, he wrote to her frequently to describe their son Waldo's newest words. Emerson undoubtedly took a special interest in these works of primal poetry, among them "mammagor," "beedy beedy," and "din din."[13] Again, we remember Emerson saying that "infancy conforms to nobody; all conform it; so that one babe commonly makes four or five out of the adults who prattle and play to it." The Danish baby video has created millions of such conformists. It is not really the particular infant to whom we give reverence by laughing our songs of praise; it is the ideal of Emersonian infancy, which takes absurd commands from a higher source, communing with that source in the process. To call it merely funny is a weak characterization.

The baby and his dad can be considered two poles in a non-foolish inconsistency in Emerson. According to literary critic Alfred Kloeckner, the "instinctive, spontaneous, and unconscious" sentiment of, in Emerson's words, "the simplicity of childhood" contrasts with an intellectual snobbery that might deny authenticity to any sentiment not also involving reflective mind and thought. Kloeckner asks whether the moral sentiment is "really the pure, instinctive, instantaneous perception which his history held it to be, or was it in practice but a partner of the intellectual faculty and at least partially dependent on it?"[14] Considering the full situation—a spontaneous baby and an intentional dad—we have resolved the dilemma. Although a baby laughing on its own is amusing, it was prompted consciously by the father, making it an absurd duet of instinct and intellect.

5. *Donating blood.* The news of violent events such as mass shootings leave people feeling a need to do something, and they sometimes fill

---

13. Quoted in Richardson, *Mind on Fire*, 286.
14. Kloeckner, "Moral Sentiment," 324.

that need through the act of donating blood. Such a gesture is not merely symbolic when blood is actually in short supply; nevertheless, because of delays in processing, the blood donated after the tragedy does not automatically end up with the people injured at that tragedy. Donating blood is thus also a symbolic gesture: your bag of blood replaces a bag from someone who donated previously. More importantly, though, there is the less philosophical symbolism of having freely issued blood replace involuntarily shed blood. Philosopher William James spoke about mandatory civil service as the moral equivalent of war. With voluntary blood donation, we have the moral equivalent of substitutionary blood atonement.

The Mississippi Valley Regional Blood Center (MVRBC), headquartered in Davenport, Iowa, provides a banquet every year to reward frequent givers. Among the rituals is honoring people according to their overall gallon count. Honoring donors from small volume to large, the accolades culminate with someone who is quantitatively the largest donor. Ceremonies are generally the only things that stand a good chance of moving me. For example, wedding receptions have a ritual dance in which couples progressively leave the dance floor according to their length of marriage. The oldest couple is left to sway on the dance floor, evoking a moral sentiment in just about everyone. After being picked off, the weaker soldiers are removed from the battlefield, and what's left are the most admirable marriage veterans. It is not just that they endured the sometimes emotional violence of marriage. It's that they simply endured the violence of life itself, hand in hand, arm in arm, and body to body.

Whereas no one dies from not being married, people do indeed die from not replenishing their lost blood. Nonetheless, the MVRBC award ceremonies do not move me at all, and in fact seem silly. I am inclined to believe that it is only a negligible sacrifice to periodically allow the pain of a needle stick and a very temporary depletion of your life force.

THE TRUE MORAL SENTIMENT

Perhaps readers reacted to these anecdotes by discovering an Emersonian sympathy with them, or perhaps they admitted a sense of disdain for some of them. Indifference is usually not an option, though. The moral sentiment demands a choice, treating indifference as disdain. For example, in 2016 NFL quarterback Colin Kaepernick was known for kneeling during the playing of the national anthem before games. The story has already been corrupted. The kneeling was a compromise from the original act of sitting during the national anthem. But this too, is not understood correctly. He did not sit; he simply remained sitting, thus refusing to stand. Technically, he did nothing, and for some minds, that was enough to condemn him.

Since this moral sentiment is so important to guiding our values and conditioning our behavior, it's worthwhile to reflect on what's behind it. When I reflect on these anecdotes, and consider any other examples presented above and below in this book, I find four salient features present in the moral sentiment:

1. individual labor for communal joy
2. immediate submission to higher power
3. communal action
4. an inexpressible appreciation

I do not think that all of these need to be present in every moral sentiment, but I do think that a full expression of the moral sentiment contains them all. Full expressions of the moral sentiment are religious in their power.

In the case of no. 1, we have something that is perhaps more political and economic than religious. But in itself I do not think it provides something that is religious. If the Cult of the Frisbee Dog fails to gain followers it will not be because of speciesism as much as because the idea is really about the appreciation of labor. And yet it will also contain no. 4, because it seems difficult to properly appreciate the labor of the dog since we know that it does not recognize the value of money and there are only so many treats it can eat. So we give it a cheer, which is to say, we produce nonlinguistic sounds out of our face.

A similar situation is present with the laughing baby and its father. The charm lies precisely in the fact that the situation is nonlinguistic. There is no reason for any of it, and we respond with inexpressible appreciation. Yet in addition, we also see another feature. The child is submitting to a higher power, innocently responding to the initiative of the father.

With the giving of blood example, we see something interesting. One is giving up part of one's body, ultimately for another individual, but more immediately for the community. Although one cannot be *legally* compelled to allow blood to be extracted from their body to be banked for the common good, they frequently are *morally* compelled to do so. This is not really a sacrifice in the sense of having to give up something important for the greater good. It is more like a kind of duty that, if one were a healthy individual, they would be petty to disregard. And yet perhaps for this reason we would not be inclined to feel an inexpressible admiration for a blood donor. In fact we would, it seems to me, see no problem in paying people to do this. We already, in fact, pay people to give plasma, and while this is usually a recourse for poor people, we do not think of it as a special tragedy that financially desperate people would have to endure, in the way, for example, they would if being incentivized for risky medical experiments. What this shows us, I think, is that blood donation is not part of the moral sentiment, since it contains none of the four characteristics.

If something is lacking in the characteristics of the moral sentiment, then any attempts to promote it would amount to a kind of aesthetic fakery. This conclusion has interesting consequences for the idea of heroism in a non-conscript military. The true moral sentiments associated with military service seem to be in decline, and this is causing an increase in attempts to promote military values, and in places such as football games. Since these are private and not national events, the playing of the national anthem serves less to promote the idea of country, and more to promote the idea of a military. We will describe this more in later chapters, but the more this militarization of values continues, the more the symbols associated with the military, when universalized to represent the country, are disclosing themselves as being fakes.

Jane Addams has an especially good view of this idea of heroism and discernment of the true moral sentiment. Despite her personal admiration for Tolstoy, she sees limitations in his writings. Tolstoy

> drags us through the campaign of the common soldier in its sordidness and meanness and constant sense of perplexity. We see nothing of the glories we have associated with warfare, but learn of it as it appears to the untutored peasant who goes forth at the mandate of his superior to suffer hunger, cold, and death for issues which he does not understand, which indeed can have no moral significance to him.

This is indeed one of the goals of art, to make moral claims without resorting to reason and argumentative battles. The problem, however, is that "it is still the appeal to dogma, and may be reduced to a command to cease from evil." This moralizing is bad enough, but "when this same line of appeal is presented by less gifted men, it often results in mere sentimentality, totally unenforced by a call to righteousness."[15] Addams' point is summed up, it seems to me, by saying that if one appeals to the moral sentiment, one better do it skillfully, or it will look fake. This is the problem with the contemporary US war-hero sentimentality. It is often depicted in an aesthetically shoddy manner, with predictable use of flags and eagles along with cliches of soldiers silhouetted on hillsides. But the individual soldier sacrificing for the good is not really the right sentiment. War represents no. 4, communal action, and not no. 1, individual labor for communal joy. The individual soldier, as Addams notes, is better expressed as an argument against war.

The reason for this aesthetic fakery is that war is not capable of drawing out the same moral sentiment as it did in Tolstoy's day. The US soldier is not compelled to fight, but rather chooses to fight. He is encouraged through advertisements, motivated with the promise of free college, and awed by the glory of war that is supported by rituals such as the national anthem and military flyovers at sporting events. And unlike Tolstoy's illiterate peasant, the US soldier has the opportunity to learn about the reasons for the war.

15. Addams, *Newer Ideals*, 6.

3

ABORTION
A Sacred Battle

Writing about abortion as a male should be, at the very least, an embarrassing project. Men should be embarrassed by other men who approach the topic from a legal and punitive perspective. For example, although I am sympathetic to Charles Michael Byrd when he asserts that "of course it goes without saying that" one should not "ignore the negative *karma* accrued by such an act,"[1] I don't think we can be that confident about the existence of such spiritual laws, much less their enforcement.

Pregnancy and birth are not experiences well suited to abstract argumentation with a crime-and-punishment focus. We can note that, in matters of warfare, men often wax sentimental about it. The sacrifices of war elicit tender emotions in men, while women's choices about pregnancy elicit tough-minded criticism from men. The obtuseness of antiabortion men has, I believe, been the biggest impediment to the antiabortion cause, and I am inclined to apply to myself the maxim I would apply to other men, namely that the best thing that can happen to the antiabortion cause is for men to shut up about it.

The existence of this book, however, would make that claim hypocritical. So instead I say that if men cannot shut up about abortion, they should at least avoid attempts to *inscribe* themselves into the debate. Philosopher Elizabeth Grosz's distinction between two types of theory about the body

---

1. Byrd, *Bhagavad Gita*, 93.

is relevant here. One of these is the "inscriptive" approach that "conceives of the body as a surface on which social law, morality, and values are inscribed." (This conception of the body seems to be shared by Kruger in her "Your Body is a Battleground" work of art.) On the other hand, there is the approach that "refers largely to the lived experience of the body, the body's internal or psychic inscription."[2] Since all bodies are sexed, according to Grosz, this means that men cannot access the lived body of a woman. They can only superimpose themselves on it. Further, she says,

> It is not really a question of blaming men but of understanding that certain perspectives are particular to their social and corporeal interests. These may not be relevant to women except insofar as they find these interests oppressively imposed on them. Many features of contemporary knowledge—knowledges based on the presumption of a singular reality, preexistent representational categories, and an unambiguous terminology able to be produced and utilized by a singular, rational, and unified knowing subject who is unhampered by "personal" concerns—can be linked to man's disembodiment, his detachment from his manliness in producing knowledge or truth.[3]

Men have to appreciate the extent to which their access to abortion is inscriptive and not lived, and further, that their own rational disembodiment—their belief that truth is a single-minded understanding—contributes to their obtuseness.

Attempts to argue, for example, a position about the "singular reality" of what counts as life occurs at a high level of abstraction from lived experience. Science, theology, philosophy are invoked to establish some fact of the matter about life and what it means to be living. Yet it remains that men simply have not had the lived-body experience of being pregnant, or the lived-body experience of someone who can be pregnant, and whose body makes a monthly demonstration of this fact. Yet is it possible to find a corresponding limitation in women? Historically, women have not had the lived experience of war. Even though there might be an increasing number of women soldiers, this does not mean that women will have the same lived-body experience as men. Boys grow up concerned that their bodies are not big and strong enough, as if they are being bred for battle—which in a sense they are, even though the battles now are more technological

---

2. Grosz, *Space*, 33.
3. Grosz, *Space*, 39.

than muscular. Boys hear war stories and receive toy weapons. The iconic plastic soldier toy that many remember from their youth included one that was supposed to be crawling on his belly. This was supposed to be a soldier sneaking under barbed wire, but boys remember how easy it was to turn him over on his back to represent a killed combatant.

Of course some girls in fact grow up playing with war toys, and some boys do not. And since women can have the lived-body experience of war, and men in principle cannot have the lived-body experience of pregnancy, men are limited to the inscriptive approach in a way that women are not. Because of this, men enter into the debate in annoying ways, invoking laws and rights and facts along with reference to preexistent representational categories intended to set the rules of discussion. Women have not usually been directly involved in the choices regarding war, and yet we cannot conclude that women should shut up about war. On the contrary, it is helpful to have outsider perspectives. And I believe it is possible for men to have a legitimate role as an outside perspective in the antiabortion cause—but only by seeing themselves as outsiders.

There is not an equivalence between the lived-body experiences of men and women. Men do not grow up being told to keep their legs together, or that they are responsible for managing the discharges of other bodies. One the contrary, men are encouraged to spread their bodies and discharge themselves on the world. So while the relationship between war-body prepping and reproduction-body prepping is not equal, there is enough of a connection of experiences to say that men can have *some* access to the experience of women and women *some* access to the experience of men. The difference, as Grosz shows us, is inscription and lived-body experience. Understood a little differently, it could be the difference between men's outside-in experience of abortion and women's inside-out experience of it.

In her *Blood Rites: Origins and History of the Passions of War*, Barbara Ehrenreich enters into the warrior mentality from an outsider position. Using the work of anthropologists, Ehrenreich suggests that the origin of war is tied to civilization protecting itself from the predation of other animals. Human hunting skills, she argues, likely derive from defensive interests. First through communal action, and then through the work of specialists on the community's behalf, humans protected themselves from predators. As the threat diminished, these specialists were left without important work. As a result, animals, and then humans, were killed for prestige. This new interest in prestige killing is essentially masculine. "War-making," Ehrenreich says,

> is not simply another occupation that men have monopolized. It is an activity that has often served to *define* manhood itself—which is exactly what we would expect if war in fact originated as a substitute occupation for underemployed male hunter-defenders. In historical times, one of the acknowledged purposes of war has been to make men "men," that is, to give the adult male something uniquely "manly" to do.[4]

War thus can be seen as a vain and pathetic attempt by men to prove their value through violence.

There is an important implication to draw from Ehrenreich here: *If war is a rite of passage for men, then abortion could be a corresponding rite of passage reserved for women.* Of course, not all women have abortions just as not all men hunt, but the ancestral habit might still persist in some.

The case of miscarriage might help to illustrate. An abortion-rights defender can note, with good reason, that abortion is not fundamentally different from miscarriage. Yet advances in health, education, and living conditions have made miscarriage less common. This formerly tragic and natural process has found a substitute in the more volitional act of abortion. What once was an event women tried to prevent is now a voluntary action. It is now expressed in the much revered woman's *choice* regarding abortion. So after men chose to make war to replace their former occupation of protecting the community against predator attacks, women who experienced miscarriage grew to believe that it was they themselves who caused the loss of life. Men could easily help condition such belief, considering their customary habit of giving specific blame to women for acts of general misfortune.

What we now value as the right to abortion is an assertion of willfulness in place of the killing that was once part of nature. Men chose to kill other men when they no longer had the responsibility of killing predatory animals. Just as women's bodies were formerly prey to natural processes (in addition to being objects for men), women came to understand these processes as the result of something they did or believed. The choice to assume responsibility for miscarriage becomes an exchange for feelings of helplessness resulting from men and nature itself.

---

4. Ehrenreich, *Blood*, 127.

So as men stopped needing to be defenders of humanity against predators, they retained their habitual violence, turning it into the voluntary violence of war. Finally, we mystify the matter by believing that wars are not voluntary at all, but rather a tragedy of nature. The process appears as a move is from no-choice to choice, and then, paradoxically, to the choice to believe that there is no choice.

It should not be denied that there are often compelling reasons for choosing abortion. From the pro-choice position, however, these reasons are not determinate causes. The woman, it is said, still has to make the ultimate decision, tragic though it might be. When one talks about tragic choices one cannot avoid thinking of the idea of *sacrifice*, an idea that unites our sentiments in the case of both abortion and war.

THE SACRIFICE OF PREGNANCY

In *War and Peace,* Tolstoy created the character of Ellen, the wife of the novel's principal character, Count Pierre Bezukhov. She marries Pierre for his money, has two affairs, and eventually becomes pregnant. Tolstoy describes this pregnancy in a way that both ridicules high-society sensibilities and shows the worst side of our attitudes about women and pregnancy. The setting is an oligarch's party sponsored by Anna Pavlovna, a Moscow socialite, where the gossip turns to a critique of the supposed illness that kept Ellen away that night:

> Everyone knew very well that the charming Countess's illness had resulted from the difficulty of marrying two husbands at the same time, and that the Italian cure lay in removing such a difficulty, but in Anna Pavlovna's presence no one dared to think of this much, much less appear to know about it.
> "I hear the poor Countess is very ill. The doctor says it's *angina pectoris.*"
> "Angina? Oh, That's a dreadful illness."
> "They say the rivals have been reconciled, thanks to the angina..."
> The word *angina* was repeated with great relish.[5]

Readers can add their own significance to the highlighted Latin word here, which happens to sound similar to the English *vagina*, or more

---

5. Tolstoy, *War*, 1086.

relevantly, to *vagin* in the French that the Russian aristocrats spoke at their *soirees*. The narrator eventually notes matter-of-factly that the Countess

> had suddenly died of that terrible malady people had found it so pleasant to talk about. At large gatherings everyone repeated the official story that Countess Bezukhova had died of a frightful attack of *angina pectoris*, but in intimate circles they discussed the details of how the personal physician of the Queen of Spain had prescribed small doses of a certain drug to bring about certain results, but that Ellen, tormented by the old Count's suspicions and by the fact that her husband (that wretched profligate Pierre) had not replied to her letter, had suddenly taken an enormous dose of the prescribed drug and had died in agony before help could be given her. Prince Vasily and the old Count were about to take proceedings against the Italian, when the latter produced letters of such a nature from the unfortunate Countess that they quickly dropped the matter.[6]

Ellen obviously overdosed on a drug meant to cause fetal death, and the gossipers don't seem much to care. The pregnant woman is cast to her lonely death. Tolstoy's novel otherwise shows that forgiveness is possible despite extraordinary differences. Pierre, for example, is reconciled to his rival, who saves him from being a prisoner of war. But no such moral grace is given to Ellen, even though it would have been possible for Tolstoy to make Pierre's wife, even despite her moral failures, into a hero herself. For Tolstoy, it seems, women's virtues are primarily sacrificial.

Ellen becomes a scapegoat for the moral corruption of the Russian aristocracy. Beneath their bantering is a perceptible sentiment of what in today's language might be called "slut shaming." Tolstoy also depicts the death of another woman, the first wife of Prince Andrei. Andrei's wife died during childbirth after having been mostly abandoned by her husband, who decided to fight in the war. Her death is presented with considerable pathos, and can be contrasted with Ellen's inglorious death, as if the *origins* of the respective pregnancies were the only relevant factor. But origins are not the important thing, because above all, both women were pregnant and deserving of sympathy and admiration. If there is a difference, it is only that Ellen chose death while Andrei's wife did not. Both were abandoned in some way.

---

6. Tolstoy, *War*, 1089.

Women can not only be abandoned in pregnancy, but also used. In Chicago, for example, the prohibition against abortion was enforced in remarkable ways. Historian Leslie Reagan researched the ways in which the invariably male police and doctors addressed deaths as the result of unlicensed abortions from 1867 to 1940. She discovered a peculiar practice in which women on the verge of dying from abortion procedures were coaxed into giving death-bed confessions in which they identified the person who performed the procedure. These confessions circumvented the legal requirement that hearsay be excluded as evidence. Reagan notes that "courts treated dying declarations as though given under oath based on the common law assumption that a dying person would not lie."[7] When people were about to meet their maker, the reasoning went, their statements had courtroom credibility. As a result of this practice though, "the investigative procedures themselves constituted a form of punishment and control"[8] tied to public shaming about premarital sex. They constituted an implicit warning to "all women that those who strayed from marriage and motherhood would suffer death and shameful publicity." Reagan acknowledges that there was more to this than just control of women. She says "historians of sexuality have given little attention to the regulation of male heterosexuality" while making an honest admission:

> I was surprised to find, the state punished unmarried working-class men whose lovers died after an abortion. The sexual double standard certainly existed, but the state imposed penalties on men, in certain unusual situations, when they failed to carry out their paternal obligations to marry their pregnant lovers and head a "nuclear" family. Unmarried men implicated in abortion deaths were, like women, punished through embarrassing questions about their sexual behavior; in general, the state punished men in more conventionally recognized ways: arresting, jailing, and prosecuting them.[9]

The point here is not that it's well and good if men were to experience the humiliation to which women have been subjected. Such a proposal is satisfying to consider, especially when one notices that, as the example of *War and Peace* indicates, Ellen's lovers were not shamed during the

---

7. Reagan, "Women," 1249.
8. Reagan, "Women," 1243.
9. Reagan, "Women," 1244.

aristocrats' parties. But punitive measures are not the only, and certainly not the most effective, way of solving social problems.

The Chicago situation gives some indication that the use of law to control bodies applies to both men and women—although not necessarily equally. The Chicago shakedown seems ultimately to be an attempt to enforce individual responsibility. "The state's interest in enforcing marriage when premarital sex led to pregnancy reveals another area where it took over the functions of the male patriarch." This could have been the partial result, Reagan says, of "feminist critiques of male sexual irresponsibility."[10]

Patriarchy was not limited to the law, however. Reagan notes that a Kentucky doctor said he "would not give testimony compromising a young lady, and I would not 'give away' a girl, but would attempt to protect her."[11] This indicates that not only is it a good idea for men to try to stay out of the antiabortion cause, but it is also wise for men to stay out of the pro-choice cause if they are doing so in order to act the part of a benevolent patriarch protecting women. The doctor appeared not to be protecting the woman's autonomy as much as protecting his idea of her modesty.

CHOICE FEMINISM AND ANTI-CHOICE FEMINISM

Philosopher Linda Hirshman is, in a way, an anti-choice feminist. In her excellent and provocative 2006 book, *Get to Work*, Hirshman argues that well-educated women choosing to stay home is both bad for the women themselves and bad for society. In a chapter titled "Feminism Could Use a Few Dead White Men," she notes that both men and women often resist any attempts by other people to advocate for better ways to live, even though "all social movements, including feminism, at its roots, ultimately rests on a concept of a good life," objectively understood.[12] Philosophers such as Plato and Aristotle saw their vocation as making people reflect on their choices. For example, according to the ancients, humans differ from other animals in their capacities for speech and reason. As Hirshman explains, a good life would thus

> include exercising the capacities that are uniquely human and those that enable people to live in groups. Those would be politics

10. Reagan, "Women," 1245.
11. Reagan, "Women," 1257.
12. Hirshman, *Work*, 31.

and philosophy, and enlightened people would display courage, piety, generosity and prudence. In a good society, people would rule and be ruled in turn so they could use their capacities both to be good governors and good citizens. Later thinkers added the value of freedom to make moral decisions, and, finally, the third standard of doing more good than harm.[13]

Hirshman argues that the first of these capacities, politics, cannot be exercised in domestic life. Although it is tempting to think of being a parent as being a political administrator, Hirshman says, justifiably, that even though bringing up kids "is important and can be difficult, it does not take well developed political skills to rule over creatures smaller than you are, weaker than you are, and completely dependent upon you for survival or thriving."[14] In short, Hirshman's argument is that a well-educated woman who chooses to stay home with her kids—and who thinks her political skills are fully employed when engaged in household management—is deceiving herself.

The second of these capacities, that of free moral decision-making, gets compromised by the domestic woman's financial dependence on her spouse. Hirshman is right again. Power resides with the person making the money, and this power is manifest, for example, in the choice of where a couple lives. Women usually choose to live in the place where the husband works. More importantly, the problem with being a stay-at-home mom is that such a woman cannot wield significant power in the relationship if conflicts arise. A woman is either dependent on her husband, or if the relationship breaks down, dependent on laws that preserve some support from him. Either way, the woman does not enjoy autonomy to the extent that the man does. Perhaps she is the ruler of the children, but the man remains in control of her.

When a woman decides that rearing the few children in her domestic sphere is more important than working to help the many children and adults found in the larger world, a woman disregards the third capacity, namely the duty to promote the greatest good. As Hirshman puts it, "the social cost of educated women's decisions to abandon their quest for positions of social power is higher than the benefit to the favored few biological offspring."[15] Society considers the nuclear family to be the traditional home

---

13. Hirshman, *Work*, 32.
14. Hirshman, *Work*, 34.
15. Hirshman, *Work*, 36.

of a woman's moral sentiments, and in following traditional philosophy, Hirschman argues that one's moral duty extends beyond the nuclear family.

Notable among Hirshman's detractors is social critic Bernard Goldberg, who includes Hirschman in his 2006 book *100 People Who Are Screwing up America*. On the subject of Hirshman's criticism of educated women who choose to be at home raising children, Goldberg says:

> Never mind that being with their young children is what they wanted to do! Never mind that many of us regard that as a job more important than working in some law firm or shuffling papers around some big investment bank! Never mind that feminism was supposed to be about *choice*! To Linda Hirshman, such a choice is simply not acceptable! ... If you ever wondered why old-fashioned radical feminism has become the butt of so many jokes and the target of so much hostility, if you've ever wondered why it is becoming more irrelevant by the day, now you know.[16]

Despite his attempt at criticism, Goldberg is actually helping to make Hirshman's point. After all, she agrees that feminism has lost relevance, but for the opposite reason that Goldberg does. She suggests that the problem with feminism involves its focus on the vague notion of choice as the supreme feminist value. In other words, it's not that feminism has abandoned choice, but that feminism has uncritically accepted choice. Hirshman lauds Betty Friedan, whose 1963 feminism had an edge that has been lost by the contemporary choice feminism inspired by Gloria Steinem. "When I poked my head above the trench of choice feminism to suggest that moral categories apply to women's lives," Hirshman notes, "I was immediately accused of trying to force women to abandon their homes and return to work. Stalinist! Nazi!"[17] Her critics confuse Hirshman's moral imperative with the idea of oppressive collectivity, when what she advocates is to use the government to ensure that women's choices to work at home are not conditioned by their financial circumstances. Goldberg appears to be perplexed by Hirshman's view, probably because he is thinking of feminism only in the Steinem way. Rather, he should be attributing the problems of feminism to the Steinem-inspired choice feminism that fails to sufficiently evaluate the choices women make.

It is not true that any choice a woman makes is by definition a feminist choice. The interesting part of Hirshman's thesis is its implications

---

16. Goldberg, *Screwing*, 100–101.
17. Hirshman, *Work*, 35.

for pro-choice positions on abortion. After all, what would the critique of women's choices mean for the choice of abortion? In a section calling for a values feminism to replace choice feminism, Hirshman goes right to the edge, saying that feminists "support *abortions* because it is immoral to abandon the poor black and Hispanic women who are the victims of the sanctimonious 'life' crowd."[18] Her position is admirably honest, and yet also close to the pro-abortion position that pro-choicers often say does not exist among women.

To be clear, Hirshman is not pro-abortion. She appears to be merely trying to remain consistent in her choice-critical position. She likely would not say that women's personal choices about abortion are irrelevant. Nevertheless, her position is consistent with the denial that a woman's choice of abortion is valuable in itself. That is, if the choice to be a stay-at-home mom is not self-justifying, as Hirschman argues,[19] neither should be the choice of abortion. Hirshman goes to abortion directly, and not just by way of choice. She says feminism supports abortions because Black and Hispanic women have an inordinate burden from pregnancy.

Conspicuously absent from Hirshman's brief statement about abortion is reference to the more privileged—and presumably more White—class of women she addresses in the book. Hirshman chides the college-bred White women who squander their personal and social potential by limiting themselves to the domestic sphere, insulated by a choice that has likely been conditioned by both chauvinist conservative men and patronizing liberal men. And Hirshman is indeed appropriately critical of both the conservative and the liberal male. It is not just the sanctimonious conservatives who are the focus, but also the protective liberals who want to shelter their spouses from the burdens of the capitalist workplace that these enlightened men supposedly disdain. After all, if work is so evil, and homelife so noble, then why aren't men choosing it more often?

It is difficult, I believe, to avoid the implications of Hirshman's view: if life choices are not self-justifying, then neither is the abortion choice. In Hirshman's view, abortion is good, not of course in the sense that women should go out of their way to have one, but in the sense that one should not be ashamed of needing one. Need, for Hirshman, is not just personal, but can be assessed as part of our deliberations about what counts as the good

---

18. Hirshman, *Work*, 91.
19. Hirshman, *Work*, 69.

life. So if we achieve a just world in which no women have an inordinate burden with pregnancy, abortion rights should be unnecessary.

This is certainly a difficult task, especially when we consider that pregnancy is a bodily commitment at some level unshareable by men. But we have found ways of compensating people for burdens, and in principle there is no reason why we cannot in a socialist world adjust matters so that the burden of pregnancy is shared equitably. If there is some additional burden that women have in relation to pregnancy that can never be addressed through the creation of a socialistic or communistic society, we would have to ask what that burden is. It is justified, I believe, to suggest that this additional burden is something other than a material in nature. In other words, if in a utopic socialist society the choice of abortion still exists, then there has to be another motivation for it. My thesis is that this mysterious motivation is that which is shared by war-minded men, and amounts to some kind of compulsion for the sacrifice of bodies.

Hirshman refers to Friedan as a first-wave feminist "trumpeter, calling women to choose something different for themselves." Friedan "likened housework to the labor of an animal." Hirshman, whose speciality is philosophy of law, says that "part of that choice became the long feminist battle over who should justly exercise the legal power to determine women's reproductive fates." She discovered that the earliest use of the term *choice* came in 1972 from an organization called Catholics for a Free Choice. (This is interesting not only because of the Catholic Church's strong association with antiabortion cause, but also because of its strong communitarian spirit.) Hirshman concludes by once again getting to edge of the matter: "saying 'choice' was initially a way not to have to say 'abortion.'"[20] It is difficult to object to her directness here.

CITIZEN RUTH AND THE ABORTION DIALECTIC

A 1996 comedy written by Jim Taylor and Alexander Payne called *Citizen Ruth* received relatively little attention. *Citizen Ruth* takes a negative approach to the issue of abortion, showing how each side is wrong rather than maintaining that one is right. The film is centered on the fictional Ruth Stoops, a poor White Nebraskan who has had four kids, all taken from her because the state maintained she was an unfit mother. Largely homeless, she is arrested after passing out from inhaling aerosol fumes, her drug of

20. Hirshman, *Work*, 18.

choice. When medical testing determines that she is once again pregnant, a male judge publically scolds her for her irresponsibility, but then privately suggests that she get an abortion. After upbraiding her by asking if she can "begin to understand the depth of your irresponsibility toward your children, toward the State, not to mention toward yourself," he then allows the charge of "felony criminal endangerment" to be applied in reference to her fetus. The philosophical battle has just been set, and what follows is a farcical portrayal of the legal issues—as well as the cultural difference—involved in the abortion debate.

Not without some genuine compassion, the judge later tells Ruth that she can "do us all a favor and [pause] take care of this problem." To make the implications clear to a demoralized Ruth, the judge speaks quietly but directly to her, with all of the clinical euphemism of an abortion doctor: "if you think you want to [pause] go to the doctor while you're in jail, you can go." He suggests that if she were to do that, he might be able to get the charges reduced.

While in jail, Ruth comes across a group of antiabortion Christian women jailed for civil disobedience, who, again not without an element of genuine compassion, respond to Ruth's despair. The public battle is now set. The antiabortion women, under the leadership of Norm Stoney of the Baby Savers activist group, post bail for Ruth and take her into their home while convincing her, through both genuine charity and moral propaganda, that she should not have an abortion. She accompanies the group to an abortion clinic protest, remaining quiet for the most part, until the harsh words directed at a woman entering the clinic elicit a middle finger of anger from her partner, who is entering the clinic with her. Ruth's instinctual response is revealing: she gives an equally angry middle finger back, showing that she is now part of the antiabortion group. For Ruth, though, her allegiance to the antiabortion cause is just a mimetic response to the pro-choice anger. Citizen Ruth is drawn into the dispute not by reasons, but through the antagonism of others.

Later, when a group of pro-choice supporters houses Ruth, she is soon convinced by their propaganda, and is told that "it is always women like you who are most *victimized* by anti-choice: indigent women, third-world women, women of color." Ruth's response is disdain: "*I'm* not a colored woman." The significance of the offense is twofold. For one, Ruth is racist, seeing herself no matter what as better than people of color. Just as important though, she is a self-sufficient White woman talking to Ruth as if she sees her as a statistic.

Bouncing between the antagonist groups, Citizen Ruth is further demoralized, and develops a learned helplessness. When asked about what she herself now believes, she says "I'm going to stay right here, and have the abortion like I wanted, 'cuz I'm a citizen, and I have my rights to, uh, pick . . . and I'm a woman, and my body belongs to me, right?" looking to her pro-choice leaders to see if she's correct. Her use of the word *pick* is more than just a reflection of her unsophistication. To "pick" is to make a relatively arbitrary choice, and Ruth is in an arbitrary psychological condition and unable to be an informed agent. Seeing her taken over by the enemy group, Norm fills in the awkward space with a characteristically male arrogance: "Your body belongs to *God*," he declares.

It is not the battles of rights that deserves the most attention in *Citizen Ruth*, but the sacrificial event that results from this clash. As Ruth continues to be courted by the two groups, she is offered monetary rewards. These appeal to her, but are disdained by the more affluent, and thus more idealistic, people on both sides of the battle. The pro-choice group in particular wants Ruth to be part of a battle and her interests to be subordinated to the greater cause. The antiabortion people make accusations of selfishness and whoredom toward her. Antiabortion protestors plead with women about to enter a local clinic, and slur-filled notes are passed to Ruth personally. And yet among pro-choice people, this is just a matter of inconsequential fetal flesh. When on the porch of the pro-choice activists' house, Ruth is told that she can have an abortion as soon as she wants, implying an abortion-on-demand policy. The next brief scene shows a bug zapper obliterating bugs.

As her scheduled abortion draws near, Ruth continues abusing drugs and alcohol, which is a direct response to manipulative pulls from both sides. Here, the movie becomes tragic. Ruth wakes one morning, sees blood on the sheets, and runs to the bathroom in a health crisis, leaving a red handprint on the door. The significance of this is perhaps not even apparent to the filmmakers. *Ruth is part of a sacrificial event.* Moses told the Jewish people to mark the doorpost with lamb's blood to be safe from the killing spree. Ruth is left to her privacy, with blood marking the door, protecting her from death. If, as Norm believes, her body belongs to God, then God seems to have evacuated the fetus from it, performing a sacrificial act in response to the communal crisis *imposed on Ruth's body*. After the miscarriage, Ruth sits in a rocking chair, serene and dignified, as if she has gone through a defining event. In chapter 7, we will see another heroic figure, Toni Morrison's Sethe, who also experiences a life-defining sacrificial act.

Overall, Ruth is somewhere between a villain, a victim, and a hero. She is the selfish whore of the ugliest form of patriarchy, and the helpless object of a patronizing feminism, and the model of feminine strength exalted by a violent and defiant feminism. She decides not to tell anyone about the miscarriage, and enters the abortion clinic in a bulletproof car, while surrounded with protesters. But she absconds through a window, taking with her the money given to her on condition that she did not have the baby. The movie's most important lesson is in the final scene: Ruth leaves the protest zone, unrecognized, as the two forces are focused on each other.

What *Citizen Ruth* shows is that the abortion debate is not just about people becoming polarized. It is also about rivalry and violent sacrifice. Ruth, and what was inside Ruth's body, were scapegoated in response to the larger problems. Men and women, pro-life and pro-choice, antiabortion and anti-antiabortion: all of them are battling each other in hopes of being able to condition her choice. After bloodshed and death, it's as if Ruth is resurrected, and then goes off into an unseen better world. She might not be a sinless sacrifice, but that is not the point. She is sacrificed, and the movie takes the side of the sacrificed and ends up presenting Ruth as a hero.

In *Pro-Life, Pro-Choice: Shared Values in the Abortion Debate*, philosopher Bertha Manninen takes on the heroic task of establishing the foundation for peace in the abortion war. She proposes that we understand both that fetal life matters, and yet that the life of the mother also matters. The life and flourishing of mothers is supported while at the same time the option of criminalizing abortion is disallowed. The result of this union is what I refer to as a tragic situation. Fetuses are both considered life and killed. Manninen says that referring to fetuses as "clumps of cells" is inauthentic. As she puts it, to regard the presence of a fetus as merely a health issue

> means we don't have to deal with the accurate statement that anti-choice advocates often repeat: that abortion really does stop a beating heart.... Although we can legitimately debate what all this means for assigning rights to fetuses, we should at least honestly acknowledge that abortion involves killing a being very unlike the terms that are typically used to dehumanize it.[21]

---

21. Manninen, *Values*, 81.

Manninen's admirable goal is to bring people together through a comprehensive acknowledgment of human dignity. The wisdom of the following is undeniable:

> Using words like *selfish* and *whore* to describe women who abort, or *tissue* and *clump of cells* to describe embryos and fetuses, encourages people to approach abortion with a dichotomous perspective and provides a psychologically easier way to deal with the uncomfortable realities that make abortion a difficult issue.... The more we dehumanize those with whom we disagree, the easier it is to convince ourselves that we are right—that we are the good guys.[22]

The result of Manninen's attempt at a comprehensive humanization becomes, as I see it, an advocacy of sacrifice. If it's not a clump of cells, it is a being with more moral significance. If the woman both acknowledges the moral significance of the fetus, and yet maintains that there is a tragic necessity to kill it, this seems like a sacrifice.

PAGLIA'S PAGAN SACRIFICE AND SCUBLA'S COMPENSATORY MALE

Literary theorist Camille Paglia is also a heroic figure. Her understanding of the abortion debate cuts through euphemism the way a military leader cuts through morality. That is, she does not shy away from the violence, and there is something undeniably admirable about this.

"The campaign for abortion rights," says Paglia in an essay titled "Sex War: Abortion, Battering, Sexual Harassment," "was systematically mismanaged by feminist leaders, partly because of their refusal to acknowledge the violence inherent in any termination of life." She continues by noting the inconsistency in abortion ethics: "The same people who opposed capital punishment ironically fought for abortion on demand, showing a peculiar discrimination about whom to execute. Squeamishly sensitive about their humanitarian self-image, feminists have used convoluted casuistry to define the aborted fetus in purely material terms as inert tissue, efficiently flushed."[23]

---

22. Manninen, *Values*, 77.
23. Paglia, *Vamps*, 49.

Paglia says her view is more consistent, since she favors the death penalty for "outrageous crimes, such as political assassination and serial rape-murder." As a function of being "fervently pro-abortion," Paglia believes "the term 'pro-choice' is a cowardly euphemism."[24] Paglia's concern for consistency is not for the sake of consistency itself. Her consistently pro-violence position in fact fails to be consistent. After all, it is unclear what is so uniquely evil about political assassinations. We can appreciate there being a relevant difference between serial rape-murder and more ordinary crimes, including single murders. But the lives of political figures are no more valuable in themselves than the lives of everyone else, and so her opposition to them seems to be arbitrary.

As for the comments on rape, Paglia invokes her "fierce Italian tradition" in which a "rapist would end up knifed, castrated, and hung out to dry."[25] She is of course being more provocative than serious, and is surely aware of the odious American lynching tradition. Generally undaunted, however, she proclaims that "you have to accept the fact that part of the sizzle of sex comes from the danger of sex. You can be overpowered." Black and Latina women, she believes, are "realistic about sex," while "these other women"—that is, privileged White women—"are sexually repressed girls, coming out of pampered homes, and when they arrive at these colleges and suddenly hit male lust, they go, 'Oh, no!'"[26] As a remedy to this pampering, Paglia exalts the "militant virgin goddesses, Athena and Artemis, with their cold autonomy." She proclaims that "evasion of nature's biological imperative is distinctly human," and lauds "abortion and sodomy for their bold frustration of mother nature's relentless fertility." She concludes that "nature's fascist scheme of menstruation and procreation *should* be defied, as a gross infringement of woman's free will."[27] She implies that women should mimic the aggression of men, and "view abortion as a sword of self-defense put into their hands by Ares, the war god." Women should allow no mediator in "our quarrel with our Creator, in this case pagan nature. . . . *The battlefield is internal, and it belongs to us.*"[28]

Paglia's ideas have some anthropological justification. They are, in fact, given support by the work of philosophical anthropologist Lucian

---

24. Paglia, *Vamps*, 38.
25. Paglia, *American Culture*, 50.
26. Paglia, *American Culture*, 57.
27. Paglia, *Vamps*, 40.
28. Paglia, *Vamps*, 41, emphasis added.

Scubla. In his book *Giving Life, Giving Death: Psychoanalysis, Anthropology, Philosophy*, Scubla identifies a way to reverse the way we think about gender relations. "Killing is equivalent to procreating in most societies," Scubla says, referring to interpretations of ethnographic evidence.

> Killing for a man is what giving birth is for a woman. By shedding blood on the field of battle, in hunting, or in sacrificial rites men try to compensate, for better or for worse, for the privilege that women possess, so long as they experience menstrual periods, of bringing children into the world. In giving death to an enemy, prey, or ritual victim, men take imaginary revenge on their mates.[29]

To some extent, revenge goes both ways. For example, we can consider the following from sociologist Gabriele Dietrich, who writes her thoughts in free verse:

> I am a woman
> And my monthly bloodshed
> makes me aware
> that blood is meant for life.
> It is you
> who have invented those lethal machines
> spreading death:
> Three kilotonnes of explosives
> for every human being
> on earth.
> I am woman
> and the blood of my abortions
> is crying out.
> I had to kill
> my child
> because of you
> who deny work to me
> so that i cannot feed it.
> I had to kill my child
> because i am unmarried
> and you would harass me
> to death
> if i defy
> your norms.[30]

---

29. Scubla, *Giving*, 144.
30. Quoted in Kyung, *Struggle*, 67.

The contrast of menstruation/life and war machines/death is apparent. There is also, however, a strong sacrificial attitude, along with a sense of determinism. Dietrich fights against male impositions of the most profound sort.

It is possible to see things another way as well. Patriarchy and violence, on Scubla's theory, are based on a pathetic jealousy. Changing the emphasis normally assigned to Freudian theory, Scubla says that "one should no longer see the child as the substitute for the phallus, but rather the phallus as a substitute for the child. It is not woman, then, but man who is marked by the minus sign."[31] Rites of passage into manhood involve attempts to imaginatively kill, and then even more imaginatively rebirth the boy without the presence of the women. And there are other, more general rituals that bear the mark of male jealousy over the procreative power of women. The Catholic priest, Scubla says, is primarily a ritual sacrificer, and his required celibacy is an especially careful precaution against mixing the blood of life with the blood of sacrificial violence. He concludes that "the blood of sacrifice, no more than blood spilled in war, cannot be allowed to come into contact with menstrual blood."[32] The key difference here is the matter of choice. Scubla notes that menstrual blood is involuntarily shed, while the blood of war is voluntarily shed. It is in this sense that maternity is natural and war unnatural (although we often are under the illusion that war is natural).

The priest represents Christ, and Christ's sacrifice has essential connections to the ideas of both voluntary and involuntary bloodshedding. Considering the idea of Christ's willing sacrifice cannot involve ignoring the fact that he was indeed killed. He gives of himself, and his self is also taken from him. He represents death *and* life, violence *and* rebirth—in short, bloodshed from the male and female perspectives.

Scubla's summary presents a pro-life alternative to Paglia's claim that "aggression must be returned to the center of feminist thinking."[33] According to Scubla,

> masculine religion sanctifies violence, sacrifice, the impure blood that irrigates our furrows: it is a religion of rites of initiation, in which men play at conceiving children by subjecting them to ordeals of blood and death: a religion of warrior gods. Feminine

---

31. Scubla, *Giving*, 282.
32. Scubla, *Giving*, 97.
33. Paglia, *Vamps*, 41.

religion sanctifies life, glorifies milk rather than blood: it is a religion of fertility cults and earth mothers, a religion of breastfeeding goddesses.[34]

The contrast of a milk–life religion with a blood–death one shows up in Toni Morrison's novel *Beloved*, as will be explained later.

---

34. Scubla, *Giving*, 285.

4

WAR
A Sacred Battle

A 1999 article in the parody magazine *The Onion* has a point–counterpoint article beginning with a young woman's thesis of "U.S. Out of my Uterus" paired with a US general's statement that "We Must Deploy Troops to Jessica Linden's Uterus Immediately."[1] Each position, it is hoped, is seen for its absurdity. On the other hand, Barbara Kruger's silkscreen art presenting a woman's face partitioned and then covered with the words "Your body is a battleground" makes a serious statement about the way we think of bodies and the value that we place on battlegrounds. I am not inclined to say Kruger's work is absurd in any sense of the word, but I would like to critique the implications of saying that bodies are battlefields.

Bertha Manninen, for example, promotes the importance of both *bodily autonomy* and *bodily integrity* in our ethical judgments. She refers to Bonnie Steinbock's thesis on the right to refuse life-sustaining treatments being derived not from a right to die, but from a "right to bodily autonomy."[2] Manninen continues by saying that such treatment "entails forcibly intruding on a patient's body with medication or other invasive treatments."[3] Similarly, she concludes, abortion is a breach of bodily integ-

---

1. *The Onion*, "U.S. Out of My Uterus."
2. Manninen, *Values*, 57.
3. Manninen, *Values*, 58.

rity, and "pro-choice advocates should focus instead on what the right to an abortion protects against: unwanted bodily intrusion."[4]

But are autonomy and integrity the same thing? Perhaps, but only if the government were requiring a woman to have an abortion, that is, if a government were so to speak inserting its forces into a body. Prohibiting the act of abortion might be an injustice, but it is not an intrusion. In other words, whatever it might be, a prohibition on an intrusion is not an intrusion. Nonetheless, Manninen, supporting the pro-choice cause, believes that intrusion is especially bad, and refers to the fact that someone cannot be compelled legally to submit an organ or blood to another person.[5] The analogy has significant limits, though. Not having an abortion is different from not being an organ donor. Organs and blood stay in the body unless extracted by external violence. The issue seems to be whether we can agree on the metaphor allowing that a law can enter the body in the way that a penis or a medical extraction device can. An antiabortion law can enter the mind, often with damaging consequences, but it cannot enter the body. The law is, to refer to Grocz's terms, inscribed on bodies, not inserted into bodies. It can be a devastating lived-body experience if the law is directed at women, but it does not have to be directed at women. A law can merely inscribe itself on the bodies of those who performed the procedures.

But laws directed at bodies are the worst response to social problems, and so I will not consider more the complications of abortion laws. I have a poor perspective on how things affect women's bodies and my arguments will be correspondingly weak here. Rather, my focus remains on the philosophy and psychology of abortion, war, and sacrifice. The conclusion from last chapter—that even the most comprehensive pro-choice position results in the situation of human sacrifice—should not escape without being investigated further. For example, human sacrifice has a significant place in Christian tradition. Theologian Stanley Hauerwas, no supporter of militarism and war, talks about human sacrifice, proclaiming that, "as a matter of fact, Christians do not believe life is sacred." Hauerwas reminds pro-lifers that "Christians took their children with them to martyrdom rather than have them raised pagan." The litany of saints who willingly sacrificed themselves speaks against the idea that all life is sacred. Some idea other than preserving life must be present. Even the idea that life should flourish is not

4. Manninen, *Values*, 59.
5. Manninen, *Values*, 29.

supported by Christian traditions that exalt the harsh asceticism of pious individuals. "To say that life is an overriding good," Hauerwas concludes, "is to underwrite the modern sentimentality that there is nothing in this world for which it is worth dying," and he adds, provocatively, "that Christianity is simply extended training in dying early."[6]

Perhaps the best statement of war and sacrifice come from Barbara Ehrenreich, who asks

> What is it about our species that has made us see in war a kind of sacrament?
> Does the fact that humans can and often do sacralize the act of killing mean that we are more vicious than any other creature? Or is it the other way around, with our need to sacralize the act of killing proving that we are deep down, ultimately moral creatures?[7]

I answer "no" to Ehrenreich's last question. In sacralizing violence, humans are neither more nor less vicious than nonhumans. They just have the capacity of deceiving themselves. Ehrenreich herself makes this implication when talking about the surprising reactions some people had to the advent of World War I. Arguing that "hardly anyone managed to maintain their composure in the face of the oncoming hostilities," she notes that many feminists "set the struggle for suffrage aside for an equally militant jingoism, and contented themselves with organizing women to support the war effort." What's more, even pacifists "felt a temptation to put aside their scruples and join the great 'awakening of the masses' prompted by war."[8] Whether one is feminist or Christian, war does often involve putting scruples aside.

CHOICE MILITARISM AND CHRISTIAN "PRAGMATISM"

Martyrs choose to die. We do not believe they are forced to die, and so their willingness for sacrifice makes all the difference. But this is an insult to martyrs, who often believe that they are *compelled* by God. Any personal choice in such a situation is inconsequential. We often inscribe the law of choice where it doesn't belong. The mere fact of choosing martyrdom is no more or less of a justification for dying than the fact of choosing to be in the

---

6. Quoted in Arner, *Bloodshed*, 47.
7. Ehrenreich, *Blood*, 20.
8. Ehrenreich, *Blood*, 13–14.

military is a justification for killing in war. If anything, the fact of choosing to be in the military could be just as much a sign of wanting to kill as choosing to be a martyr is a sign of wanting to die. So considered, the issue within Christianity is not the *choice*, but the *action*, and the action is to be involved in violence. As Rob Arner wisely concludes, "There are many things worth dying for in the suffering love of Jesus, but nothing worth killing for. To me, nothing is worth the idolatry and presumption of taking into my hands that which only God may give."[9]

Whether or not one is Christian, there is always a tendency to invoke religious language in speaking about pacifism. For example, Jane Addams, along with Leo Tolstoy, eschewed doctrinal religion in favor of a prophetically pragmatic faith in human welfare. Yet Addams nearly gives a sermon when she speaks about the attitudes of the Russian peasantry, proclaiming that

> the religious revival which alone would be able to fuse together the hostile nations, could never occur unless there were first a conviction of sin, a repentance for the war itself! As long as men contended that the war was "necessary" or "inevitable" the world could not hope for a manifestation of that religious impulse which feeds men solely and only because they are hungry.[10]

Addams invokes the idea of sin, and then refers to the Matthew 25 text in which Christ appears in heavenly splendor—only to recommend that the key to salvation is, in the apt words of literary critic Terry Eagleton, "an embarrassingly prosaic affair"[11] involving feeding, clothing, and otherwise taking care of ordinary people. Addams and Tolstoy understood this, and thus separated the sheep and the goats by distinguishing the patriotic bread-labor of peasants from the false patriotism of regime and government worship. As for Addams, she says that "men are instinctively wary of accepting at face value high sounding claims that cannot justify themselves by achievement."[12] Elsewhere, she criticizes shallow idealism, saying that people "die willingly only for a slogan."[13]

People also are willing to die for those who merely mouth the slogans. In Tolstoy's *War and Peace,* there is this revealing description of the mind

9. Arner, *Bloodshed,* 47.
10. Addams, *Peace,* 126.
11. Eagleton, *Meaning,* 165.
12. Addams, *Peace,* 120.
13. Addams, *Peace,* 57.

of the young Count Rostov, who beholds the face of his leader, Emperor Aleksandr, addressing the troops before battle. "Everything about the Tsar," says the narrator, "seemed to him entrancing," and "he longed to express his love in some way, and knowing this was impossible, he was ready to weep." This oddly romantic impulse is changed into a sacrificial one in the young man's heart, and he feels himself to be willing to die for the leader, exclaiming internally, "'How happy I would be if he were to order me to throw myself into the fire this instant.'"[14] Rostov's youthful idealism and clarity is soon met by the dirty moral business of the battlefield, where the pulls of patriotism and natural self-interest serve to fragment the soldiers' wills. They are torn between the moral impulse to advance and the natural impulse to retreat. After the battles come to favor the advancing Napoleon, Rostov's hero Aleksandr becomes a compromising pragmatist, negotiating a peace with the enemy force. At an awkward ceremony in which Napoleon gives an award to a Russian soldier, Rostov is perplexed, and experiences a clash of ideas and sensory reality. As Tolstoy's narrator describes it:

> So vividly did he recall the stench of putrefying flesh that he looked around to ascertain where the smell was coming from. Next he thought of the self-satisfied Bonaparte with his white little hand, who was now an Emperor, liked and respected by Aleksandr. For what, then, were all those severed arms and legs, those men killed?[15]

The white gloves cannot cover up the deaths. And what does it mean that two prominent men can show such respect for each other when the men who were actually fighting were only allowed to see each other as mortal threats?

Unfortunately, Tolstoy's Christian anarchism remains an aberration. The militarism and determinism of modern humanity are developing at a demonic pace. Militarism has infiltrated our minds so that we see war as inevitable, something human and natural and yet, paradoxically, beyond human control. In *Between the Eagle and the Dove: The Christian and American Foreign Policy*, political scientist Ronald Kirkemo proclaims that "we cannot expect the world to be changeless, and we cannot expect nations to be talked out of their historical aspirations and ideological convictions." He says that these nations can be "given the choice of no satisfaction

---

14. Tolstoy, *War*, 207–8.
15. Tolstoy, *War*, 477.

of their goals at all or relative satisfaction by mutual compromise."¹⁶ As Kirkemo describes it, a nation with pacifist aspirations will fare poorly. After all, there is a tendency for countries to "slip into a Machiavellian policy of simple power calculation and a moral pragmatism."¹⁷

Although giving a responsible hearing to the pacifist position, Kirkemo capitulates to militarism. He invokes "tyrants" in Nazi Germany and Stalinist Russia who have "commonly debased persons in particular and people in general" to conclude that

> a Christian does not have to like wars or support all wars. There are different kinds of wars and different kinds of evil. And to allow the complete triumph of one evil in order to completely refrain from another is not responsible. The pacifist is right in abhorring the killing of war. But the pacifist ethic ought not be applied in an absolute fashion to all times and circumstances.¹⁸

It is unclear, however, why a Christian could even consider the violence of tyrants as a complete triumph. Christian faith is the belief that evil can never ultimately triumph. Kirkemo allows tyrants to triumph. If nothing else, Christ's resurrection represents a belief that, no matter what appears to happen, evil has not and will not win. It is not that Christianity magically redefines victory in the face of defeat (as Nietzsche, for example, might say); it is that Christianity is in perpetual opposition to the evil of tyranny *and* violence. It gets knocked down, and rather than turn itself into a lesser evil, it raises itself up to be a perpetual witness against all evil.

THE CULT OF BLOOD ATONEMENT

In her book *Cults in our Midst*, psychologist Margaret Thaler Singer writes about what she calls "cultic relationships" in which "a person intentionally induces others to become totally or nearly totally dependent on him or

---

16. Kirkemo, *Eagle*, 52.

17. Kirkemo, *Eagle*, 18. Here, Kirkemo brings out one of the common, mistaken meanings of pragmatism: the willingness to impose one's desires on others at any cost. This counterfeit idea of pragmatism seems to be derived from a metaphysics that places the mind as the initiator of action and the body as its servant. In the political sense, this is similar to the idea of a ruthless authoritarian, who plows his intentions through the world, concerning himself little with moral resistance. When Benito Mussolini famously claimed to be a pragmatist, it was more likely in this sense. The general idea seems to be one of ends justifying the means, or rather, arbitrary ends justifying cruel means.

18. Kirkemo, *Eagle*, 85.

her for almost all major life decisions."[19] This definition is adequate except that cults are not necessarily based on a dependence toward one individual. And Singer herself makes a distinction between cults and a controlling organization such as the United States Marine Corps.[20] The Marines Corps, she notes, is a voluntary organization that one can in principle choose to leave.

I would offer that the idea of being voluntary is not applied particularly well in cases like these. After all, feelings of loyalty are strong, and volition is restricted by considerable psychological limitations. For example, it seems like we freely choose compliance to patriotic traditions such as standing for the national anthem. Yet the results of not standing are strong social disapproval. "Please stand and remove your hats . . ." is not really a request. If you wish not to stand it is better that you move away from those who are, because they do not believe you should really have a choice in the matter.

A cult is not merely a group that challenges a legitimate tradition, and it is not necessarily a group that focuses itself on one individual. Rather, cultic relationships are ones in which people are united through a mutual acceptance of violence. To be in a cult is to participate in a tradition of violence and use that tradition as justification for that violence. My example is from the history of The Church of Jesus Christ of Latter Day Saints (LDS), but I am not implying that LDS in general is a cult. I am arguing, rather, that this example shows how justifications for violence are found within the culture of the United States.

In a foundational story from the *Book of Mormon*, the prophet Nephi undergoes a moral trial. "Led by the Spirit, not knowing beforehand the things which I should do," Nephi approaches the house of Laban, who is lying drunk and unconscious nearby. Taking Laban's exquisite sword, Nephi is overcome by a profound feeling:

> And it came to pass that I was constrained by the spirit that I should kill Laban; but I said in my heart: Never at any time have I shed the blood of man. And I shrunk and would that I might not slay him. And the Spirit said unto me again: Behold the Lord hath delivered him unto thy hands. Yea, and I also knew that he had sought to take away mine own life; yea, and he would not hearken unto the commandments of the Lord: and he had also taken

---

19. Singer, *Cults*, 7.
20. Singer, *Cults*, 98–101.

away our property. And it came to pass that the Spirit said unto me again: Slay him, for the Lord hath delivered him into thy hands; Behold the Lord slayeth the wicked to bring forth the righteous purposes. It is better that one man should perish than that a nation should dwindle and perish in unbelief. (1 Nephi 4:11–13)

Laban is drunk with the genius of wine, while Nephi is encountering a spirit of violence. It is not difficult to see the similarities between the two men, each ambitious and overcome with a mysterious force. We witness in this story two aspects of the ancient Greek story of Dionysus: drunkenness and homicide. Nephi first had to overcome his understandable compunctions about killing, and then "took Laban by the hair of the head, and I smote off his head with his own sword." Then, in a predictable move, given the similarities between the men, Nephi says he "took the garments of Laban and put them upon mine own body . . . and I did gird on his armor about my loins" (4:18). This is an act of superficial theophagy. He is not consuming the god to get its power, but he is impersonating it, putting its skin on his body rather than its flesh in his body.

As in the case of God speaking to Abraham in the *akedah* (i.e., Genesis 22) there is a mysterious and unethical imperative being given. And so even when we agree Laban did the things attributed to him, we should have some pity for him, just as we should for the son Abraham was about to sacrifice. In both cases, a defenseless man gets killed because of a directive from the Beyond. The conclusion of the *akedah* is not really a happy one: A lamb gets killed; a son is terrified. The conclusion to Nephi's slaying of Laban is no happier, and in one sense more troubling. Abraham is humbled by the experience before a terrible God. Nephi, on the other hand, takes on the identity of Laban, subsequently impersonating the murdered foes to deceive Laban's servants. By killing Laban, Nephi becomes a Killer Laban.

As early as 1886, the LDS was under suspicion of practicing what was called "blood atonement." It was believed that Mormons who committed grave sins such as murder were subjected to secret executions. According to Joseph West, people believed Mormons cut the throats of violators. This supposed punishment, done outside of ordinary American law, drew a committee investigation in the US House of Representatives. West's testimony to the committee was that, according to his experience in Utah, "the Mormon people do not execute any such penalties against anybody, or any other penalties; that for violations of church laws, members are simply excommunicated from the Church, and nothing more"[21]

Our concern here is with West's defense. In response to the "blood-curdling stories" of rumor-filled newspapers, he said that "there is nothing secret in the doctrine, its theory or practice. At most, it is but a logical and pure continuation of the belief of all Christians in Christ's sublime atonement for the sins of a fallen race." That West would see this as a natural extension of Christian doctrine is troubling in its implications. West continues: "We do not accept hanging as the fulfillment of the sacrifice; because by that death the murderer's blood is not literally shed." Yet this is all theoretical, since, as he says, "we distinctly disavow any individual or church right to execute that plain law of necessary blood-atonement." For him and the church, "the belief is merely passive." The following passage reveals more than it intends:

> Is there anything blood-curdling in the belief that a merciful God will sometime give to men the opportunity to die in the flesh, by the swift stroke of a righteous vengeance, rather than to suffer eternally in the spirit? Those persons who are shocked by such a doctrine cannot truly understand the significance of Christ's death. *For if it be a horror for a guilty body to be broken in behalf of its own spirit, how much more of a cruel injustice to command a divine and sinless soul to suffer the agony of crucifixion to atone for a fall not His own!*[22]

The argumentative move here is remarkable: if you are offended by the idea of someone dying because they committed murder, you should be more offended by the idea of someone dying *without* having committed a murder. So since you are not offended by the premise of Christianity—that Christ died for something he didn't do—you shouldn't be bothered by the idea of murders being executed. West is unwittingly exposing the "cruel injustice" of the substitutionary theory of the atonement. If we do happen to be offended by capital punishment, we should be at least as offended by vicarious capital punishment. The problem here is that West assumes no one would be offended by the idea of capital punishment. Mormons do not deny the implications of violence and vicarious atonement, says West, but they deny the "monstrous absurdities" that have been falsely claimed "in

---

21. J. West, "Blood-Atonement," 643.
22. J. West, "Blood-Atonement," 644–645, emphasis added.

the practice of that principle."²³ So it seems that West claims—with unintentional irony—that Mormons are to be credited for not actually following their principles.

For those interested in moving away from mythological justifications of war, there is hope in the form of an article by Mormon scholar Josh Madson, who challenges tradition by reading the *Book of Mormon* as saying, at least in spirit, that war does not solve anything. Bravely, he asks whether the book is "the witness of the survivors," or "the witness of the bodies crushed under the weight of their own civilization"? He advocates that the testament be read as literature rather than just literally, thus removing the mystification about violence. The story line of the *Book of Mormon* begins with foundational violence and leads to problems that are only solved by the intervention of Christ's revelation. Madson's prophetic statement is that violence comes from "the fundamental values of a society that are both rooted in mythic accounts of national beginnings and essential to national unity."²⁴ His remarkable conclusion is that

> Like the Nephites, we can no longer repeat false narratives without risking destruction. We cannot justify our national sins by citing Nephite wars. If we want to emulate Book of Mormon peoples, let us emulate those who were able to escape their cultures' narratives and find another way . . . laying down their weapons and like Christ offering themselves instead . . .²⁵

Madson's message might have difficulty being heard. In 2003, LDS President Gordon Hinckley told Mormons that if they must go to war, "they should go with love in their hearts for all God's children, including those on the opposing side. Then, if they shed another's blood, their action will not be counted as sin."²⁶ Historian Richard Bushman agrees, but notes that even the stipulation that wars must be defensive is not strict, if only because "everyone believes that they are going to war to defend themselves. The terrorists even believe they are defending themselves against American aggression."²⁷ It appears, then, that while the LDS story begins with Nephi's bloody decapitation of an enemy, perhaps it will end with sympathy for the

---

23. J. West, "Blood-Atonement," 645.
24. Madson, "Non-Violent," 23.
25. Madson, "Non-Violent," 28.
26. Quoted in Bushman, ed., *Awakening*, 3.
27. Bushman, ed., *Awakening*, 2.

enemy, which would mean understanding that enemies are often doing the same thing we are.

So in sum, LDS is not a cult, but in its history it shares with the larger culture a cultlike dedication to the necessity of violence and sacrifice. If we are to look for cultlike characteristics, we should look not at relatively small and unfamiliar groups, and project secret acts of evil on them. The cult in our midst is more likely to be the United States' military–industrial complex, which is large, persistent, and producing ever new justifications for its actions.

WAR, SPORTS, AND SACRIFICIAL HEROES

Generally, it is difficult to keep sports fans quiet in a stadium, but when "The Star-Spangled Banner" is being played, there is a tacitly enforced silence among the crowd. An announcer asks for hats to be removed, and sometimes requests we call to mind soldiers who have made sacrifices. The communally sung lyrics speak of war and endurance. The crowd can fail to notice that the last line is a question rather a declarative statement: "Oh say, does that Star-Spangled Banner yet wave o'er the land of the free and the home of the brave?" Is the question about looking for the flag, or wondering about the character of the land on which it stands? People assume that they stand on stable moral ground and are just looking for the flag as validation.

Bravery is a virtue that is powerful in evoking our moral sentiments. Yet if a soldier is to be considered brave, then a risk-taking peacemaker should be considered braver, at least within a Christian culture. In the largely Christian United States, though, the soldier seems to be considered the highest hero. Among these, the sacrificed soldier is higher than the surviving soldier, but the surviving soldier is still considered a strong moral authority. In some cases the US soldier is not just considered a moral authority, but almost a savior. "Only two defining forces have ever died for you. Jesus died for your sins, and the American soldier died for your freedom," says a recently developed American proverb, which has shown up on internet memes. Christ and soldiers are naturally connected through the idea of sacrifice, but in this specific case there is an important boundary that is crossed. The soldier kills; Jesus does not.

But the idea apparently elicits a moral sentiment in some people. And the slogans that arise often have a powerful force, especially in context of war. Writing shortly after World War I, Jane Addams argues that an abstract statement, necessary in all political relationships, becomes greatly intensified in times of war, as if illustrating the contention that men die willingly only for a slogan. . . . Had the slogans—this is a war to end war and a war to safeguard the world for democracy—become so necessary to united military action that the Allies resented the naive attempt on the part of the Russian peasants to achieve democracy without war? They so firmly believed that the aims of war could only be accomplished through a victory of the Allies that they would not brook this separation of the aim from the method. Apparently the fighting had become an integral part of the slogan itself.[28]

Addams shows the sacrificial nature of war, one in which it is believed necessary for unity. "The making and unmaking of these myths," says Addams of the Russians, "always accompanies a period of great moral awakening."[29] The same applies to myths in the present century. Perhaps the most prominent of these myths is the belief that US soldiers have died to defend US citizens' freedoms. Considering this myth puts us into what I will call the Freedom Fighter Free Speech Paradox. To explain, we return to the situation of NFL quarterback Colin Kaepernick choosing to sit out the national anthem in protest during part of the 2016 season, which caused patriotic Americans to be instinctively offended. Debate often focused on a commonly invoked question: Is it appropriate for someone to disrespect soldiers when the very freedom to disrespect soldiers came from the efforts of those soldiers? Each side believes it is on solid logical and moral ground. The supporters of the soldiers believe it is contradictory to protest that which gave one the right to protest. The protesters believe it is contradictory to criticize someone who is using, in its most general sense, the right the soldiers supposedly gave to them.

The debate itself involves differing levels of abstraction about the ideas of freedom. We do not seem to get particularly offended by contradictions, unless there is something concrete at stake. No one dies from someone either sitting or standing at the national anthem. The debate is framed on the soldiers having already died. If one had to take sides in the abstract dispute, then the protesters are probably right. It is a worse contradiction for freedom to deny the exercise of that freedom, than for freedom to disrespect the supposed source of that freedom. In any case, it is surely no contradiction for freedom to fail to publicly honor those who are believed

28. Addams, *Peace*, 57.
29. Addams, *Peace*, 55.

to have been sacrificed for freedom. What must be noticed, however, is that both sides share an unjustified presumption, namely that American soldiers have in some concrete way been defending Americans' freedom of speech. Without evidence of concrete threats to that freedom, and concrete causal connections between the death of the soldiers and the end of that threat, this assumption is unwarranted, and the belief is guided only by our imagination and rationalization.

In her discussion of the origins of American religion, theologian M. Gail Hamner speaks of the "Puritan imaginary," a term she draws out of the work of post-Freudian psychoanalyst Jacques Lacan. The imaginary, she explains, is related to what Lacan called the mirror stage, understood as the time an infant first sees itself in its reflection.

> The moment of recognition occurs when a baby grasps that the image in the mirror is indeed an image of itself. Analogously, the moment of recognition occurs when a person identifies with a nation's flag. For both examples, the recognition is always also a misrecognition. The image in the mirror is not actually the baby, and the flag is not actually the person.[30]

Hamner wants to trace the changing ideal of Puritanism in the American Imaginary, her name for the "various mechanisms of recognition, misrecognition, displacement, and mediation whereby nineteenth-century citizens understood themselves to be American."[31] If we were to give a name to the twenty-first-century American Imaginary, I would offer that it be called the *Military–Idolatrous Complex*.

This imaginary tells us that we fight wars for ideals when we really fight for concrete interests. In *War is a Force That Gives Us Meaning*, Chris Hedges notes that soldiers in battle focus on tasks "of cleaning weapons, of readying for the business of killing. No one ever charges into battle for God and country." A Marine Corps lieutenant colonel about to enter Kuwait told Hedges that none of the "boys is fighting for home, for the flag, for all that crap the politicians feed the public. They are fighting for each other, just for each other."[32] Hedges also explains that, for non-soldier citizens operating under the "nationalist myth," "the collective glorification" permits them "to abandon their usual preoccupation with the petty concerns of daily life."[33]

30. Hamner, *Pragmatism*, 11.
31. Hamner, *Pragmatism*, 12.
32. Hedges, *Meaning*, 38.
33. Hedges, *Meaning*, 54.

The whole matter of idealizing soldiers disturbs me not because I have a problem with soldiers. Rather, it is more that I notice in myself a reflex to explicitly tell people that I do not have a problem with soldiers. In few other contexts would this come up. If I had a problem with businessmen, I could express it freely; if I had a problem with priests I could say it openly. No one feels especially compelled to distinguish the valor of the businessman from the bad system that he was put in. One could say he is pursuing his self-interest, but so are some soldiers.

The difference here is not difficult to see: soldiers, unlike the others, risk their lives. Yet they are also taking lives. The COVID-19 pandemic has created a new hero, the healthcare worker, but it remains to be seen whether this valorization will reach the stage where it is taboo to critique them. They are essential workers, since disease is a natural enemy. Soldiers, however, are not essential workers because war is a *moral* evil, which is to say, it is something that would be eliminated from our world if we chose to do so.

Sacrificed soldiers are hallowed, and surviving soldiers are considered sages, almost on all matters. In many ethical debates, from those of life-and-death relevance to those of psychological well-being, everything seems to be filtered through the US soldier. For example, in convincing people not to set off fireworks excessively, we appeal the concerns of veterans with Post-Traumatic Stress Disorder. Simple civility, that is, the belief that our current orgy of explosions around July 4th is disrespectful to neighbors who do not like loud noises, is insufficient. Nor is pointing out that the play violence of fireworks is a disrespectful simulation of real violence. It does not require PTSD to be upset by the presence of simulated bomb explosions made mostly by people who have never themselves experienced real ones.

To consider a similar situation, we have to return to sports, and note what happens when the imaginary violence of sports turns real. For example, during a 1991 football game, Detroit Lions lineman Mike Utley fell directly on his head, breaking his spine underneath almost 288 pounds of body mass. He was paralyzed from the chest down and, determined to be physically self-reliant, he set a goal of one day symbolically walking off the football field. He said that "a man walks on the field of battle, and he walks *off* the field of battle."[34] The hope was to conduct a special ceremony at which Utley would walk under his own power in the midst of a group of Detroiters. That it has not yet happened does little to devalue the story. He

34. Eno, "Utley."

is still heroic, a Sisyphus perpetually forced *not* to move. The idea of Utley's public walk, practically meaningless but spiritually significant, calls forth a moral sentiment, and his comment about battle deepens it if we interpret it in a certain way. To walk off the field of battle means that the warrior has avoided death. The best way for all soldiers to walk off safely is if the battle stops.

As another example, we stay in Detroit and move to a different sport. During a 1998 Detroit Red Wings hockey game, the intensity of competition was stopped for a moment as former defenseman Vladimir Konstantinov arrived in the arena. Konstantinov had been seriously injured in a car accident six days after winning the 1997 Stanley Cup. He spent several weeks in a coma with head injuries and paralysis, in addition to significant neurological damage. With considerable physical limitations—Konstantinov was wheeled onto the scene in a wheelchair—he managed to make a thumbs-up sign to the crowd. Something in his motions suggested to the viewer a loyal animal response, much like a dog lifting its paw to shake a human's hand in an awkward way. Adding to the scene was the sight of the players below, many of them from the opposing team, making the customary gesture of tapping their sticks on the ice in respect.

Discovering another layer of moral sentiment, we notice the fact that Konstantinov was known as a premiere goon—a player whose skills focus on hard-checking and otherwise physically intimidating opposing players. Hockey goons are the berserkers of sports, unleashed to provide explosive force to the regulated battle. The historical context of this small event was the memory of the Cold War, itself transcended in this moment of sympathy for the injured goon, who in times past would have been feared, hated, and reviled.

Joyce Carol Oates describes the transcendence provided by sports in a pithy philosophical book called *On Boxing*. Oates writes that "the triumphant boxer is Satan transmogrified as Christ, as one senses sitting among a delirium-swept crowd." The boxer, like athletic heroes in general, is "a bearer of inchoate, indescribable emotion—a savior of sorts, covered in sweat and ready for war. But then most saviors, sacred or secular, are qualified by a thoughtful 'of sorts.'"[35] How does one explain this qualification? Perhaps the boxer discloses the violence within the voluntary activity of sports, while soldiers mystify violence in the presumed necessary activity of war. Oates says that for her the appeal of boxing is complex, and common

---

35. Oates, *Boxing*, 153.

terms like "enjoyment" and "brutality" are misapplied. She does not think of it as a sport, nor "in writerly terms as a metaphor for something else." It is not "a symbol for something beyond itself," as an "abbreviation" or "iconographic." In "this struggle on an elevated platform enclosed by ropes . . . in the presence of an impatient crowd," identities merge, with "you and your opponent so evenly matched it's impossible not to see that your opponent is you." Oates concludes with philosophical power: "Life is like boxing in many unsettling respects. But boxing is only like boxing."[36]

In his novel *End Zone*, Don DeLillo makes a similar point. The book is ostensibly about a college football team, but is really about war. It is not a simple matter of football being a metaphor for war, though. As a character named Zapalac says, "I reject the notion of football as warfare. We don't need substitutes because we've got the real thing."[37] DeLillo's characters describe how the event is "gladiatorial" because "they fatten us up and then put us in the arena together. They train us to kill, more or less." This killing is done unconsciously, accidentally, and the narrator describes, flatly, how he was "one of three players converging on a safetyman who had just intercepted a pass. We seemed to hit him simultaneously. He died the next day and I went home that evening."[38] The three meet in violence in order to negate the one. The sacrificial element is made explicit in one of the characters, who wears a sweatshirt with the schools' symbol, a screaming eagle, under which is the word "SACRIFICE."[39] This goes along with the somewhat odd verb that the narrator notes is being found all around town: "MILITARIZE."[40]

Sacrifice and militarization thus seem to go together naturally. Zapalac gives further prophecy about the danger of "patriotic manifestations."

> Let me just simply mention flag-waving and the insane ritualizing that goes on every time a flag is hiked up a pole or some veterans of Gettysburg come hobbling along with their medals, their stickpins, their poppies, their flags, their hats, their banners, their bumper stickers, or some simple sports event where you look up suddenly and there's sixteen thousand Shriners and Masons with their comical Turkish hats and they're covering every inch of the

---

36. Oates, *Boxing*, 4.
37. DeLillo, *Zone*, 164.
38. DeLillo, *Zone*, 22.
39. DeLillo, *Zone*, 24.
40. DeLillo, *Zone*, 20.

playing field with, in the middle of them all, three hundred and eighty-five high school girls dressed in red, white and blue who are prostrating themselves on the cold earth as they assume the shape of an American flag being dragged through yak dung by syphilitic foreign students and off to the side there's some crippled television personality on a wheelchair and pulleys singing the national anthem as the cystic fibrosis child of the month poses in the nude for the cover of *Life*. I tend to worry about such spectacles.[41]

Zapalac's sardonic depiction of the culture of war, patriotism, and sacrifice is just as evident today as it was forty years ago. What has noticeably increased, however, is the link between war and technology. A quarterback, it is said, should be tall because "they can peer over the curvature of the earth in order to spot their receivers."[42] Aerial warfare, so common today, is even more remote.

Another professor, this one justifying his existence by teaching ROTC, notes how war in fact actualizes technology. "Your technology doesn't know how good it is until it goes to war," he says, "until it's been tested in the ultimate way. I don't think we care too much about individual bravery anymore. It's better to be efficient than brave."[43] In fact, "weapons technology is so specialized that nobody has to feel any guilt. Responsibility is distributed too thinly for that. It's the old warriors like myself who have to take the blame for what the so-called technocrats and multi-dimensional men are up to."[44] And yet he believes that eventually there will be "humane wars" in which "each side agrees to use clean bombs, and each side agrees to limit the amount of megatons he uses." When it happens, "there'd be all sorts of controls. You'd practically have a referee and a timekeeper. Then it would be over and you'd make your damage assessment." In addition, however, he notes that "a war may have to be fought; it may be unavoidable in terms of national pride or to avoid blackmail or for a number of other reasons."[45]

Wars do not *have* to be fought, and they certainly do not need to be fought for national pride. To believe that national pride is a determining cause of war is like mistaking the moves in a game for actions in reality. Part of the essence of a game is the knowledge that the activity is voluntary.

41. DeLillo, *Zone*, 164–65.
42. DeLillo, *Zone*, 165.
43. DeLillo, *Zone*, 84.
44. DeLillo, *Zone*, 86.
45. DeLillo, *Zone*, 81–82.

When Zapalac says football is the real thing, this is more than just a form of playful postmodern inversion of values. It is saying the truth. Football is the real thing because, unlike war, it is aware that it is fake.

5

GOD HATES WAR
The Accidental Prophecy of Westboro Baptist Church

In his review essay "Religion, War, and the Meaning of America," Harry S. Stout argues that the "encompassing and collective question of who we are as a nation (singular) of war is not raised. Nor, relatedly, is the question of religion's contribution to the nation of war."[1] My goal is to use the Westboro Baptist Church (WBC) as a way of raising that question.

But even to mention WBC is to commit a sin. The church founded by lawyer Fred Phelps and his family has been on a unique mission. The group is not intending to change minds. As Calvinists, they realize that only God changes minds, and he does so capriciously. What they are doing is a test, and blessed are those who are not offended by them.

Few seem to be so blessed. Progressives are offended by WBC's criticism of homosexuality, conservatives are offended by its criticism of military service, and everyone is offended by the manner in which it does this criticism. In a 2003 episode of the Fox News debate show *Hannity and Colmes*, the following exchange with WBC member Shirley Phelps Roper highlights our difficulty with WBC:

> **Hannity:** Do you feel good about going to funerals of men who have put their lives on the line for their country in order to give you the right to do this, and to inject pain into their families' lives?

---

1. Stout, "Religion," 280.

Phelps Roper: I feel good about warning this country that the wrath of God is pouring out on their heads, and that they will not obey, and that the Lord your God is punishing this nation . . . and one of his weapons of choice is sending your children home dead from the battle . . .

Hannity: Obviously you're a nut. . . . You are as mean, and as sick, and as cruel, as anyone I've ever had on this program, and the fact that you use religion to justify your hatred this way is frankly mind-numbing . . .

Phelps Roper: There are no innocent people, thank God for 9/11, thank God for dead soldiers, thank God for IEDs . . .

Colmes (interrupting): Shirley, this is Colmes, Shirley . . . What's the matter with you?[2]

What is remarkable here is not just that the conservative Hannity and the liberal Colmes are united in opposition to Phelps Roper, but that each of them is so flustered in his attempts at rebuttal. This befuddlement is emblematic of America's difficulty in processing WBC intellectually and understanding it morally. A country that bears an ambivalent relationship to its Puritan past is likely to have difficulty with a group like WBC that claims to be Calvinist in its philosophy, and yet decidedly anti-American. How can something be religious and so unpatriotic? When Colmes asks "What's the matter with you?" it should not be thought of as just a rhetorical question—an act of verbal violence—but an attempt to understand. I believe we are not particularly clear in articulating what it is that makes the demands of WBC seem so small and these people so insignificant in our moral considerations.

In other words, there are a number of ways, ultimately inadequate, that we try to reject WBC:

1. WBC is crazy. This is the first and easiest response, but also the most mistaken. Many of those in the Phelps family are lawyers, versed in argumentation. All of them are amateur Bible scholars, and extraordinarily familiar with the text. Crazy people say incoherent things, but, if anything, WBC is hyper-coherent, with everything cohering to the Bible. The beliefs of WBC are so strong as to be nearly unfalsifiable. Anything said against it is taken as a sign of Satan's influence, and bolsters WBC's sense of righteousness. After all, the Bible literally says that the truth will undergo persecution. To argue from any position

---

2. Phelps, at 2:00 to 2:30.

other than the literalist reading of the Bible is to be corrupted with sin, and amounts to a persecution of the truth. The more offensive WBC becomes, the more response it gets, and this response is viewed as persecution, which in turn corroborates the theory that the truth must be persecuted. As maddening as this type of reasoning is, it is not so much crazy as intellectually irresponsible. Perhaps what is really meant by saying that WBC is crazy is that it is morally reprehensible in some way that we cannot quite explain. To further articulate, we can try three other responses.

2. WBC is too mean-spirited. This is perhaps the most common, and in a way understandable criticism. It amounts to the belief that WBC is causing too much harm by what it is doing. The WBC response is simple: If it is mean, this is only because God is mean. The group's website includes copious examples of biblical passages, not all of which are from the Old Testament, indicating that God is wrathful. On their appraisal, God's final wrath is infinitely worse than the hearing of any offensive slogan that WBC might utter. An ethical calculus always works in favor of WBC here, at least from their perspective: preventing what it takes to be the certainty of eternal torment outweighs the near certainty of temporal offense. This reasoning seems even to work with people skeptical about the existence of hell, or of God's willingness to send people there. After all, the mere possibility of eternal torment should outweigh the near certainty of temporal offense. Early American Puritan Jonathan Edwards would occasionally give sermons with fearful effects. His notorious "Sinners in the Hands of an Angry God," generally noticed for the individualistic terror it tries to elicit, also includes what can be interpreted as a call for social sympathy:

> If we knew that there was one person, and but one, in the whole congregation, that was to be the subject of this misery, what an awful thing would it be to think of! If we knew who it was, what an awful sight would it be to see such a person! How might all the rest of the congregation lift up a lamentable and bitter cry over him![3]

Those used to hearing Edwards preach about God holding humans like dangling spiders over the fire of hell would be surprised to

---

3. Edwards, "Sinners," 27.

find Edwards also arguing, in *The Nature of True Virtue*, for what he calls benevolence to being in general, as the true virtue. Such benevolence is not limited by any spheres of private interest, including that of country or empire. In fact, he notes, "among the Romans, love to their country was the highest virtue; though this affection of theirs so much extolled, was employed as it were for the destruction of the rest of mankind."[4]

The main point of Edwards's moral theology is to identify "a propensity and union of heart to being simply considered,"[5] and such a propensity is Edwards's way of talking about Christian love. WBC, in a way that seems perverse to many, thinks it is reproving people in an act of love. It believes it is enduring persecution to warn people who have become so deaf to biblical truth that such truth needs to be yelled at them with a bitter cry. This belief that extreme danger warrants extreme warnings leads to consideration of another general criticism.

3. WBC is too extreme. This criticism is only a little different from no. 2, but rather than focusing on the politeness of the belief's expression, it is more focused on the belief itself in relation to mainstream theology. The WBC response would be simple: true Christianity is extreme. Mainstream Christianity, they would argue, ignores Bible passages condemning popular sentiments and advocating narrow paths. And, what's more, the fact that something is extreme does not entail that it is wrong. That to which it is considered extreme might just be in the wrong.

4. WBC fails to distinguish the sinner from the sin. This view tends to be held by mainstream conservative churches, who wish to agree with, for example, WBC's criticism of homosexuality, while still being bothered by the mean-spiritedness of this criticism. This view is a more formidable criticism and seems like it would be supported by Cornel West, at least in a general sense. Speaking about Martin Luther King Jr., West says that nonviolent resistance to evil is to be "directed at the forces of evil, rather than against the persons who commit the evil. The enemy is injustice and oppression, not those who perpetrate the injustice and oppression."[6] The response to the criticism that WBC

---

4. Edwards, *Nature*, 88.
5. Edwards, *Nature*, 8.
6. C. West, *Reader*, 432.

should distinguish sinner from sin is that those who are proud of their homosexuality are not themselves making such a distinction. Indeed to say that one should distinguish oneself from one's sexual attractions is considered offensive by many people, and anti-gay speakers can be harshly criticized for claiming that homosexuality is a choice, and thus amenable to change. Sexual identity, however, is generally thought of deterministically, and the attempt to distinguish sinner from sin becomes a form of disrespect. The somewhat disturbing, but nonetheless reasonable conclusion here is that WBC respects homosexuals more than mainstream conservatives do. After all, at least WBC hates them for who they truly are.

Literary theorist Michael Cobb deals with WBC by proposing the "'queering' of religious hate speech about queers." Religious hate speech, he says, "does not necessarily only hurt and harm." It has other uses, and "queers also mine the hostility and politics of the old and very traditional rhetorical forms of national belonging" in order to pervert the intentions of those who utter such speech and even promote a greater awareness and acceptance of homosexuality.[7] Cobb's work is excellent, and deserves further consideration as a way of dealing with the demands of WBC. The focus here, however, is on a different aspect of the appropriation of WBC's message. What follows is an attempt not to queer WBC's message, but rather pacifize that message. To do so, we have to look at the group as providing a challenge to the American consciousness that is different from the one apparent to most people. In short, I believe WBC challenges the valorization of war in US culture.

ANTI-WAR CALVINISM

Appropriating the Calvinists for new purposes has a place in US intellectual history. Cornel West, for example, considers the African American gospel as one that "lauds Calvinistic calls to transform the world, yet shuns puritanical repression."[8] He picks from the Puritans what he thinks works best for his idea of deep democracy, and neglects what he thinks works against it. This eclectic style of pragmatism is neither irresponsible nor unprecedented. It has roots in US thought, with Benjamin Franklin as a noteworthy

7. Cobb, *God*, 9.
8. C. West, *Reader*, 439.

example. According to philosopher James Campbell, for Franklin, "the Puritans' interest in self and in salvation as the core of personal piety was replaced by the call for virtues like industry, frugality, and duty that were unconcerned with any demonstration of election and fostered in the place of this concern efforts to advance human well-being."[9] Herbert Schneider writes that Franklin "made the attempt to maintain the Puritan virtues in all their rigor, but to abandon entirely their theological sanctions,"[10] including those involving temperance, not only for eating and drinking, but also for general "inclination or passion."[11]

What is it, then, that we can take from a contemporary expression of Puritanism such as that of WBC? Unlike what Franklin would do, I believe we should understand WBC religiously. I would prefer, in fact, to take the religiousness of their message and abandon questions of virtue. We do not need to regard those in WBC as examples of Puritan virtue; rather, we need to regard them as prophets—but in a way different from what they themselves would have us believe. We should regard WBC as a group serving, as all prophets minimally do, to present challenges to an otherwise unreflective community. In the case of the United States, WBC serves to challenge Americans' unreflective valorization of war, their belief that war is inevitable, and that war is an appropriate expression of patriotism. The US valorizes its soldiers over its people, celebrates military functionaries over human beings, advocates violence over love, and, looking at it from a more distinctly Judeo-Christian perspective, places nation above God. We can understand WBC the way that Henry David Thoreau might. With words that are famous but apparently underappreciated nowadays, he proclaimed that:

> The mass of men serve the State thus, not as men mainly, but as machines, with their bodies. They are the standing army, and the militia, jailers, constables, *posse comitatus*, etc. In most cases there is no free exercise whatever of the judgment or of the moral sense; but they put themselves on a level with wood and earth and stones; and wooden men can perhaps be manufactured that will serve the purpose as well. Such command no more respect than men of straw, or a lump of dirt. They have the same sort of worth only as horses and dogs. Yet such as these even are commonly esteemed good citizens. Others, as most legislators, politicians,

9. Campbell, *Recovering*, 99.
10. Schneider, "Puritans," 144.
11. Schneider, "Puritans," 146.

> lawyers, ministers, and office-holders, serve the State chiefly with their heads; and, as they rarely make any moral distinctions, they are as likely to serve the devil, without *intending* it, as God. A very few, as heroes, patriots, martyrs, reformers in the great sense, and *men*, serve the State with their consciences also, and so necessarily resist it for the most part; and they are commonly treated as enemies by it.[12]

Presenting their message in their military funeral protests, WBC serves God without intending it. Granted, WBC's early notoriety came from protests at the 1998 funeral of a gay man believed to be the victim of a hate crime, and it also has protested gay pride events, Jewish community centers, the funeral of heavy metal vocalist Ronnie James Dio, and indeed anything else it believes intolerable. The group is most notorious, however, for its protests at military funerals. Perhaps this is because it is here that the WBC triggers a deep reflex in the American nervous system, one that has developed from origins in violent revolution, has been traumatized through Civil War, and now extends itself into a global military presence—one that nearly always justifies itself through relatively vague but nonetheless heartfelt declarations about the preservation of freedom.

WBC deserves at least some comparison with other provocative voices in contemporary America. Cornel West strikes a deep nerve when he says that in American popular sentiment, "the flag is no longer subordinate to the cross, the cross has become subordinate to the flag." He then mentions the Reverend Jeremiah Wright, a religious figure who like Phelps is considered divisive. Wright "terrifies the white mainstream. When he says, 'Not God bless America, God damn America. That's in the Bible, for killing innocent people.' The white mainstream only hears, 'God damn America!'"[13]

WBC of course is notorious for its similar claim that God has damned America. In the following passage from West, the difference between him and WBC depends merely on how one understands the word "injustice":

> Any God worthy of worship condemns injustice anywhere. To be anti-injustice in America is not anti-American! If to condemn injustice in America is to be anti-American, so be it. To be Christian requires being maladjusted to injustice, which is the bottom line.[14]

---

12. Thoreau, *Disobedience*, 10.
13. C. West, *Hope*, 80.
14. C. West, *Hope*, 81.

For West, injustice involves economic disparity, as well as racial, ethnic, and sexual identity discrimination; for WBC, injustice involves failure to follow God's laws, particularly those forbidding homosexuality. The methods used are similar, differing only in that WBC is bolder, by not only preaching directly into the face of those they believe need to hear it, but doing so at a time that these people seem least to want to hear it. WBC attended a 2011 Memorial Day service at Arlington Cemetery in Washington, DC, and drew predictable counterprotests. Most interestingly, among these were people identifying themselves with the Ku Klux Klan, which, prior to the arrival of WBC, was perhaps the most hated group in America. CNN presented a revealing, and quite frankly amusing, dialogue between the KKK and WBC.

> "It's the soldier that fought and died and gave them that right to free speech," said Dennis LaBonte, the self-described "Imperial Wizard" of the KKK chapter that he said he formed several years ago.
> "That's fine," said Abigail Phelps, the daughter of Westboro Baptist Church founder Fred Phelps. "They have no moral authority on anything."
> "People like them say it's white power . . . white supremacy," Phelps said. "The Bible doesn't say anywhere that it's an abomination to be born of a certain gender or race."
> LaBonte insisted he is not a racist nor a "hate-monger," but said he believes the white race is "slowly and most assuredly being denigrated."[15]

Each group is attempting to take the moral high ground for all to see. LaBonte expresses the belief of Hannity, and indeed that of most of the US, when he refers to soldiers fighting for freedom. I do not believe there is anything disingenuous about LaBonte defending the troops; it seems, on the contrary, to be just a natural extension of his pro-America beliefs, themselves an extension of his pro-White beliefs.

For LaBonte, Hannity, and the ordinary American, the problem seems to be that WBC is blaspheming some sacred institution by denigrating the men and women beatified by that institution. Yet one can see this level of veneration of the troops as an example of idolatry, or at least misdirected sentiment. An example of this is in the holiday of Memorial Day, which, in its common observance, does not only involve memorials of people, but

---

15. CNN, "Counterprotestors."

also an implicit valorization of American warfare. The symbol of Memorial Day is the American flag, not American citizens. The faces of those who died are not made primary focus, and when they are, these people are usually shown in military attire. Another example of misplaced sentiment involves the celebration of Mother's Day, which is quite different from its original intention by Julia Ward Howe, who saw it as an anti-war protest from mothers of Civil War casualties. Her original proclamation calls not for mimosas and brunch, but for a moral act of defiance:

> Say firmly:
> "We will not have questions answered by irrelevant agencies,
> Our husbands will not come to us, reeking with carnage,
> For caresses and applause,
> Our sons shall not be taken from us to unlearn
> All that we have been able to teach them of charity, mercy, and patience.[16]

An attempt to return Mother's Day into an edgy day of protest against the valorization of militarism surely would encounter resistance. Doing something similar with Memorial Day, for example, by refusing to acknowledge military virtue, or by acknowledging enemy soldiers along with the Americans, would encounter fierce resistance. In America, there is understandable regret for lost lives, but little regret of war.

WBC celebrates war and all of its dead, and US society thus vilifies them, largely for failing to respect the difference between the people and the cause. If this is objectionable on the part of WBC, however, should it not also be objectionable on the part of military families? It is rare to find a memorial for a dead soldier that does not involve the displaying of a US flag. It seems a little unfair to blend love of country with love of persons, venerate these things simultaneously, and yet also expect critics of the country to respect a boundary between them. If WBC does not have the moral high ground by failing to distinguish the person from the soldier, then neither do American families, who also fail to make such a distinction, although for different reasons.

To be sure, WBC has never said its goal is to be critics of military idolatry. WBC's *Open Letter to Lawmakers on Legislation Regarding Her Counter-Demonstrations at Funerals of Dead Soldiers* tries to make it clear that:

---

16. Howe, "Proclamation," 82.

> We aren't anti-war protesters; we aren't anti-don't-ask-don't-tell protesters; we're the prophets of God. We don't care who's in office; we don't care about your politics; we don't care about your policies on the war. The fact is the American public will never know the truth from its politicians about how this war started or what's really going on in Iraq. The other fact is that there are a variety of viewpoints among Americans and Iraqis about whether we should be at war; the purpose of the war; and how it's going. All of that is irrelevant to us. The simple fact of the matter is this: This war had to happen; Bush has to be persuaded to stay in this war; America had to become Babylon. This is the means by which God is punishing America, and nothing is going to change that fact.[17]

It is difficult not to see this as anti-war prophecy, even despite its statement to the contrary. WBC is not concerned with which political party started the war, and why. It believes the war would be inevitable no matter which party was in power. A consideration of American history, in which wars have been instigated by both parties, fails to discredit this claim. "Put bluntly," says Stout, "the American consensus consists in America's faith in the institution of war as a divine instrument and sacred mandate to be exercised around the world."[18] The WBC challenge is directed to America, and in particular to those within its mainstream religious culture.

ANTI-WAR PRAGMATISM

War punishes all countries, no matter who "wins." They get punished most powerfully in the form of, as Roper Phelps said, "sending your children home dead from the battle." WBC's position is not incompatible with the claim that war deals a heavy blow to the world, not just a particular country. If members of WBC were to say that we should thank God for dead Iraqis, they would be making the same point (although it is revealing that such a statement would, from the point of view of the KKK, as well as that of other patriotic Americans, be something to celebrate). WBC, by not taking sides in the war, is indicating that there is no such thing as a good side to war. God sees all, and God hates war. WBC says God damn America and, in this situation, it becomes difficult for Cornel West, Jeremiah Wright, and

---

17. Westboro Baptist Church, "Letter," 3.
18. Stout, "Religion," 284.

indeed every other person especially critical of American militarism, to disagree. Imagine being given the following text anonymously:

> Several months ago the media began reporting on the funerals of soldiers killed in Iraq (or occasionally in Afghanistan). Theretofore, the media had been in *pari delicto* (equal fault) with President Bush and his administration in pretending no one was dying in these wars. Then the tide turned, and the media began reporting on the funerals. The stories portrayed public events, with strutting soldiers, marching bands, flag-waving, America-worshiping and peals of self-pity and human worship spread all over the public sidewalks. It became clear that the media, military, and families of these dead soldiers were using the deaths of these young men and women to promote their agendas, and impose upon the American people at large their Godless views about the war and the deaths of these soldiers.

The word *Godless* marks this as religiously based anti-Americanism, but provides little other evidence of its source, be it a conservative church or a left-leaning activist group. The text continues by noting that, once the media began reporting more about the war,

> people puffed out their chests, thumped them long and loud, waved that dishonorable ignoble filthy fag American flag, and screamingly demanded that God bless them.[19]

In this last part of the diatribe—which is indeed taken from the WBC's "Open Letter"—there is but one three-letter slur that marks this as being from WBC and not an angry anti-war activist.

WBC members are, after all, activists. This claim might be strange, given that the group is also decidedly Calvinistic. One might wonder why it is preaching against US sin if the fact of that sin is predestined. Why try to change the world if change is not within our control? Answering this question brings out the psychological nuances of American thought. There is a tendency, for example, to think of wars as inevitable. As noted in chapter 1, William James speaks about the common view of war as "a sacred spiritual possession worth more than all the blood poured out."[20] People think of it as "a biological or sociological necessity, uncontrolled by ordinary psychological checks and motives."[21] Using Calvinist notions of determinism,

---

19. Westboro, "Letter," 2.
20. James, *Heart*, 162.
21. James, *Heart*, 166.

James makes a psychological point, in effect criticizing this war-hawking determinism. Such a belief in determinism has convinced people that war and sacrificed soldiers are inextricably tied to American freedom. "Freedom isn't free" says the common American in defense of military action, and in support of determinism.

Even Calvinistic determinism has its cracks, however. There is an implicit place for action within it, and it is at this point that pragmatism begins. Perry Miller expresses the situation clearly:

> What is hard to get moderns to comprehend about the founders of New England is, first, that for them the doctrine of predestination did not have as a psychological consequence the surrender of all volition but rather that it was a powerful stimulus to activity; second and more important, this tremendous exertion being made in a social context, the incentive was therefore strengthened by an awful realization that without it the whole enterprise might fail.[22]

Within a deterministic theology that assigns people *a priori* to either heaven or hell, it might appear there is no motivation to do anything. New England Calvinists, however, could not know with certainty about their destiny. They had to consider various signs of election, and these involved things such as charity toward others, diligence in business, humility, and willingness to preach the gospel. Whether or not these were theologically part of one's essence, one was still free, practically speaking, to do these activities and cultivate these virtues. Metaphysical beliefs did not get in the way of people trying to give themselves indication of their election through engagement in activities deemed valuable. So there is room for voluntary activity in Calvinism, even if this voluntary activity is just what goes on when theology winks and then turns away from what people actually do.

I believe it possible that WBC is doing a similar wink. Despite their claims about America's foreordained decrepitude, Margie Phelps, speaking before the US Supreme Court, stated her group's message clearly. Speaking of soldiers, she says: "Nation, hear this little church. If you want them to stop dying, stop sinning."[23] This is remarkable in two ways. First, it implies that there is hope for America; second, it involves an interesting logical claim. Phelps appears to be saying that, if the deaths stop, then it was because you stopped sinning, and in particular, because you stopped the supposed sin of tolerating homosexuality. But when will American military deaths ever

22. Miller, "Resolution," 235.
23. Associated Press, "High Court."

stop? Given that both political parties tend to support war, the antecedent will never be true, and thus the conclusion is irrelevant. We should, rather, take from WBC a different message: Nation, hear this little church. If you want them to stop dying in war, stop sending them to war. Such a message might be tautological, but it has prophetic importance.

Jesus says to "love your enemies, do good to those that hate you, bless those who curse you, pray for those who abuse you. If anyone strikes you on the cheek offer the other also" (Luke 6:27). For WBC, love means experiencing public condemnation in order to warn people of God's wrath. This can be granted to them, and if by expressing their form of love they are thought an enemy of common decency, then we are obligated not to respond with violent actions, or violent words, or even, as is the case with the revving Harley Davidsons that show up, the violence of superior decibels. The demands of WBC, for better or worse, are a fact to be addressed, so we still must do something with WBC, for WBC is determined to continue. We will take their words to mean that, when all is said and done, it is really war itself for which we are accountable to God. If WBC will not accept this theory, it is our prerogative, and perhaps even our duty, to impose it on their words and actions, for as it is written, "do not be overcome with evil, but overcome evil with good" (Romans 12:21).

Emerson believes that goodness must have an edge to it. This does not mean that all edgy things are good, but rather that all good things are edgy. I will not claim that WBC is, all things considered, a good thing. I will claim, however, that they are admirably self-reliant. America's reaction to them—whether it is a reflexive cry against them or an honest evaluation of its own values—will determine the goodness.

6

HARD CHOICES
Violence and Sacrifice in Toni Morrison's Beloved

At the beginning of this book, I cited Dorothy Day about the beauty of a child being born amongst the tragic situations of war and poverty. The story was intended to be as much a critique of war as it was an exaltation of motherhood, as Day challenges us to lower the status of the killing heroes while raising up the birthing heroes. Men are traditionally the killing heroes, while women are both traditionally and naturally the birthing heroes. As Scubla argued, men have historically killed because they have been biologically incapable of giving life. And as Ehrenreich argued, men kill other men in wars because they are no longer killing predatory animals, as they did in more primitive communities. Building on these conclusions, I propose that a woman's choice of abortion can be conditioned by the larger context of male violence.

Men take life as a response to the fact of giving life. In one sense, this is understandable. Men protected pregnant females from external danger. But in another sense, it is not defensible. Men should not be killing because of their insecurities about their own inability to produce life. So two things are providing the context of abortion: the idea of protection and the idea of killing as a response to failure. Abortion, in this sense, becomes the symptom of a deep social problem. Abortion can be a reaction against the male privilege of killing. At heart, this claim does not contradict the pro-choice feminist position that sees abortion as integral to the defense of women's autonomy in the midst of male domination. The claim presented here is,

I hope, also congruent with Manninen's idea of finding shared values in the abortion debate. Whatever we think about abortion, it is not a matter without significance, and cannot be relegated to a choice abstracted from the cultural context involving moral sentiments of violent sacrifice.

In this chapter, we further consider this topic by considering how male privilege develops through distorted ideas of heroism. We consider Toni Morrison's 1988 novel *Beloved,* which I see as showing us how historical sentiments of racism and sexism in the US lead to choices of sacrificial violence. To explain, I consider the novel in relation to the *akedah* that we considered briefly in chapter 4. The Genesis 22 story of Abraham binding his son Isaac is similar to the story of Sethe's killing of her daughter. Abraham attempts to sacrifice his son while acting on a moral imperative that is difficult for an outsider to understand. A comparable situation is present with Sethe, but *Beloved* shows that Sethe is not as fortunate as Abraham. As we will see, she is not restrained in her attempt and has to live with the consequences of her choice. *Beloved* can thus be seen as not only an exposition of the effects of slavery and racism, but also as a critique of race and gender privilege. Morrison's narrative style highlights the differences between the stories: *Beloved* is presented in a way that does not allow the reader to escape from consideration of the concrete situation of moral choice.

SPITE AND BABY VENOM

When encountering the Genesis 22 story of Abraham's attempted sacrifice of his son Isaac, the reader is put in a position of historical privilege, particularly when the version of the Bible they read includes subheadings. Oftentimes the story—referred to as the *akedah*—is framed with the title "Abraham Tested," allowing the reader some psychological ease. This amounts to what we might call a "spoiler," and the reader is actually happy to have the story spoiled for them. If Abraham's predicament was *just* a test, after all, Abraham could never ultimately have had to go through with the murder. Yet if it were not marked as a test, the reader would naturally put themselves in the place of Abraham, experiencing the anguish and uncertainty he undergoes after receiving the mysterious imperative. The matter-of-fact narrative style of the Bible does not convey this anguish, and makes it seem like Abraham was always poised in the decision:

> He said to him, "Abraham!"
> "Here I am," he replied.

HARD CHOICES

> Then God said, "Take your son, your only son, Isaac, whom you love, and go to the region of Moriah. Sacrifice him there as a burnt offering on one of the mountains I will tell you about."
> Early the next morning Abraham got up and saddled his donkey.
> (Genesis 22: 1–3)

The sparse narration offers possibilities for historical embellishment. For example, God's repetitiveness is perhaps a response to Abraham's hesitation or willful ignorance to what he clearly hears. It's not that Abraham doesn't hear what is said, but that he doesn't know who or what said it. After all, it could be the result of insanity, or ultimately the devil tricking Abraham by speaking as if he has authority. To stall, Abraham might have asked "Are you referring to this son, or the other one?" In response, God has to be exceedingly clear and unambiguous. What appears to be merely a poetic repetition—"your son, your only son, whom you love"—is also part of a tragicomic dialogue in which Abraham anxiously avoids the choice and God has to hammer home the meaning.

Perhaps Abraham also had questions about the source of the statement. After all, it is not characteristic of God to demand such a murder. How does one determine the essential identity of someone except by the character they display? Merely hearing a voice you believe is God is insufficient. For example, in the heresy trial of religious hero Anne Hutchinson, the accused exploits this ambiguity to the point where she convicts herself before the Puritans: "How did Abraham know that it was God that bid him offer his son, being a breach of the sixth commandment?" she asked. "By an immediate voice," responded the court, to which she immediately rejoined "So to me by an immediate revelation."[1] The dangerous implication of the words were clear, and Hutchison confirmed the Puritan suspicions.

Hutchinson is right, though. The voice that Abraham hears is immediate, that is, mysterious to outsiders. But Abraham cannot *know* whether the source of the voice is good, and can only act in a way that is indistinguishable from insanity. Knowing the "happy" ending, we do not have to be frightened: it was, after all, *only* a test; Isaac was spared.

Morrison's *Beloved*, however, offers the reader no such privileged position of knowledge. It begins cryptically, and the reader is drawn into the story before knowing what it's about.

---

1. Morgan, *Puritan Dilemma*, 152.

> 124 was spiteful. Full of baby's venom. The women in the house knew it and so did the children.[2]

Beloved alienates the reader with an allusive insider style that withholds information. ("124," it turns out, is the house number.) The women know what is going on before the men do. Eusebio Rodriguez calls this the beginning of "narrative shock tactics,"[3] more shocking to those who have not themselves experienced similar historical trauma. The narrator then begins "releasing the story slowly," so that "listeners and readers are persuaded to accept Beloved as a "presence" in a story of "haunting significance."[4] This is largely why Catherine Gunther Kodat calls the 1998 movie adaptation of *Beloved* "wretched," having "trivialized the novel by turning it into a horror film—a genre that, despite its manifest unreality, employs narrative devices grounded in literary realism."[5] A similar movie about Abraham would have similar problems. There is no booming voice of God to establish righteousness, and, at any rate, why would a boom establish anything? Readers of Genesis are led into the story as if making their way up a mountain. Readers of *Beloved* are led down from that mountain, to a sad house of reclusive souls.

Eventually readers encounter the protagonist Sethe in her most tragic moment, having decided to kill her daughter rather than have her subjected to slavery. I argue that important parts of *Beloved* take on a new significance when understood in light of the *akedah*, and, more important, that the *akedah* is subjected to a well-deserved critique by Morrison's presentation of the story of *Beloved*. Abraham attempts to sacrifice his son while acting on a moral imperative that is difficult for an outsider to understand. Sethe, however, is not as fortunate as Abraham. She lives with what Eddie Glaude calls the "pragmatic view of tragedy" that demands that we "look at the tragedy of our moral experience straight in the face, and, with little certainty of the outcomes"—that is, no spoilers to the story—"*humbly* act to make a better world for ourselves and our children."[6]

Glaude is right about the uncertainty of outcomes, but Sethe is no more humble and ameliorative than Abraham was. Neither person's act of sacrifice made a *better* world, but only continued the violence. As for

2. Morrison, *Beloved*, 1.
3. Rodrigues, "Telling," 153.
4. Rodrigues, "Telling," 161.
5. Kodat, "'Garner,'" 162.
6. Glaude, *Shade*, 44.

Sethe, her unfortunately successful sacrifice results in a significant tragedy rather than an immediate redemption. She is subjected to consequences from which Abraham was spared, illustrating, I believe, a second level of social injustice to that of slavery itself. *Beloved* takes the *akedah* in a new and more tragic direction by using a protagonist of a different race and gender, and creating an ending in which an opprobrious act of sacrifice is not prevented by a transcendent force. Morrison is not trying to show that women slaves had it worse than men slaves; on the contrary, her novel poignantly highlights the terrible effects of slavery on both sexes. I believe, however, that *Beloved* can be seen not only as an exposition of the effects of slavery and racism, but also as a critique of moral privilege, especially as it relates to male agents who believe they enjoy the greater safety of God in their lives. According to Gurleen Grewal, *Beloved* shows that "memory's journey into the individual and collective past becomes the means of self-knowledge, catharsis, forgiveness, and release."[7] But in *Beloved*, it is unclear that the end justifies the means.

SETHE'S SILENCE

Sethe does what she believes is right, despite being set apart from the human community as a result. Her name, according to Dana Medoro, suggests the pre-Egyptian god "Seth," who is "set against the permanence and tyranny of existing orders."[8] Sethe's self-defining moment comes through her most troubling action, one in which an immediate decision puts her beyond ordinary morality, while still tragically subjected to the punishments required by that morality. Jan Furman notes that "punishment for crimes, even righteous ones, is obligatory in Morrison's fiction,"[9] thus giving Sethe's action not only an element of tragedy, but also civil disobedience. Jean Wyatt offers that Sethe "extends her rights over her own body" to "her children, folding them back into the maternal body in order to enter death as a single unit." Yet for the children, there is no going back. The ethics are complicated, and Morrison herself refers to Sethe's choice as "absolutely the right thing to do, but it's also the thing you have no right to do."[10]

7. Grewal, "Memory," 142.
8. Medoro, *Bleeding*, 156.
9. Furman, "Re-memories," 268.
10. Quoted in Wyatt, "Body," 214.

BODIES AND BATTLEFIELDS

Beloved's most dramatic scene takes place in a barn, where Sethe is confronted by her former owner, referred to merely as "schoolteacher," and three other men, including a local sheriff. The narrator speaks of them as the "four horsemen,"[11] indicating that the end has come for her freedom, and that justice is being manifested. This justice is of course controversial, since the men are attempting to return Sethe and her family to the South in accordance with the notorious Fugitive Slave Act.

After her older children had fled with other members of her slave community, Sethe was left to venture north on her own while pregnant. She gives birth to her youngest daughter, Denver, while crossing the Ohio River on the way to meet her family. When she is finally reunited with them in the free North, the family embodies a new life of freedom for Sethe and, by symbolic expression, the African American people emerging from slavery's degradation. Yet upon the approach of the reclamation crew, Sethe slits her older daughter's throat, and tries to kill her other children. Approaching the barn, the horsemen see that

> inside, two boys bled in the sawdust and dirt at the feet of a nigger woman holding a blood-soaked child to her chest with one hand and an infant by the heels in the other. . . . Right off it was clear, to schoolteacher especially, that there was nothing there to claim. The three (now four—because she'd had the one coming when she cut) pickaninnies they had hoped were alive and well enough to take back to Kentucky . . . were not.[12]

Former slave Stamp Paid "snatched the baby from the arch of her mother's swing," thus acting like the restraining angel who saved Abraham from evil. One of the reclamation team, the nephew of schoolteacher, is perplexed by the behavior of Sethe. "What she want to go and do that for?" he says.[13] The nephew had viewed her as a mere animal, and, in an earlier scene, had forcibly nursed from her breast as an act of confused adolescent dominance. Now, it seems to him, she is a peculiar type of animal.

Eventually, the infant is given back to her mother—a living child exchanged for a dead one—and Sethe, with blood on her nipple, nurses the baby anyway. As the narrator notes, the prevailing opinion among the reclamation team was that Sethe is "testimony to the results of a little so-called freedom imposed on people who needed every care and guidance

---

11. Morrison, *Beloved*, 148.
12. Morrison, *Beloved*, 149.
13. Morrison, *Beloved*, 149–50.

in the world to keep them from the cannibal life they preferred."[14] And yet in order for Sethe to be considered moral, she also has to be held to a moral standard exclusive to humans. The sheriff's summative words to the three slave owners are important here: "'You all better go on. Look like your business is over. Mine's started now.'"[15] The job of reclaiming property is over; the job of considering matters of human justice begins. The belief that negroes are objects gives way to the belief that negroes are agents, since only agents are subject to legal penalties. Thus, as Sethe is led out of the barn, the narrator describes her with a certain ironic admiration. She has, indeed, through the terrible act, also given herself freedom. She is no longer an animal; she is a moral agent.

> Holding the living child, Sethe walked past them in their silence and hers. She climbed into the cart, her profile knife-clean against a cheery blue sky. A profile that shocked them with its clarity. Was her head a bit too high? Her back a little too straight?[16]

Morrison shows that Sethe's act is self-defining. It determined the rest of her life, since she now has been allowed into human morality, along with its legal consequences. One does not prosecute property, after all. In another sense, though, she has transcended human morality. The mysterious imperative upon which she acts is beyond full comprehension. Terry Otten says that Morrison does not want the reader to forget "the awful truculence of her deed," one that is "understandable but not excusable."[17] One could, with as much justification, say that the deed is excusable more than it is understandable.

Morrison herself says that the total absorption of mothers in their children can be "understandable," but "excessive."[18] Paul D, Sethe's romantic partner later in life, cannot cope with finding out what she had done. Hearing her say she did it to protect the children, he remarks that her love is "too thick," to which she replies "Love is or it ain't. Thin love ain't love at all."

> "There could have been a way. Some other way."
> "What way?"
> "You got two feet, Sethe, not four," he said.

---

14. Morrison, *Beloved*, 151.
15. Morrison, *Beloved*, 150.
16. Morrison, *Beloved*, 152.
17. Otten, *Crime*, 82.
18. Quoted in Darling, "Realm," 252.

The narrator quickly notes that "right then a forest sprang up between them; trackless and quiet."[19] Paul D had, probably unintentionally, accepted the oppressor's system of classification, placing Sethe among the animals.

Also important to note is the symbolism of trees. Treated like a beast of burden, Sethe has a beating scar on her back that is interpreted as looking like a chokecherry tree. The scar came as the result of her speaking out about schoolteacher's nephew taking milk from her. For literary critic Sandy Alexandre, this tree scar serves to show that the violence against Black women is at least as significant as the violence against Black men, whose injustice is represented in the lynching tree. "If black male and female oppression stem proverbially from the same tree," she asks, "then how is it possible that black male oppression makes headlines in ways that black female oppression never has nor can?"[20] Morrison, she argues, is trying to highlight the kind of specifically misogynistic violence and degradation that has been relatively neglected in the story of slavery.

Glenda Weathers goes so far as to relate the "death-dealing trees" of Sethe's plantation home with the biblical tree of knowledge. This home, however, "seemed to the male slaves a virtual sanctuary—a prelapsarian world in contrast to other plantations."[21] Sethe sees things differently, having a deeper and less constructive memory. The tree-filled gap that arises between Sethe and Paul D represents not only the difficulty that men have in understanding the thickness of women's memory, but the difficulty that *anyone* has in understanding Sethe.

A forest also separates Abraham and Isaac from everyone else. The three-day hike involved leaving first the wife and mother, and then the servants. In a similar way, Sethe's decision, and Paul's insensitive response, indicate that she has left the world behind. Her decision places her beyond a morality that considers life itself more important than circumstance, and she considers the ethics of the world less important than mysterious imperatives. Additionally difficult to understand is how Sethe is able to be self-possessed in the midst of such a decision. *Beloved*'s unidentified narrator—who often represents the voice of the community—questions the appropriateness of her proud poise while being led away.

For his part, Paul D likens her to an animal, an act of substitution that allows him to avoid thinking about the problematic moral situation with

---

19. Morrison, *Beloved*, 164–65.
20. Alexandre, "Tree," 917.
21. Weathers, "Biblical Trees," 206.

which she was confronted. This problem is expressed in the haunting question: Is it better not to live than to live as a slave? When Sethe, by her violent actions, answers yes on behalf of her children, we can see her poise of self-possession as either that of a defiant murderer, or that of a moral hero. The narrator, otherwise rather harsh and exclusive, concludes with a question: "Was her head too high and her back too straight?" Was she, ultimately, a hero or a villain? The same question needs to be asked of Abraham as well.

ABRAHAM'S SILENCE

Søren Kierkegaard's *Fear and Trembling* brings out the troubling lack of firm distinction between murderers and moral heroes. Writing through the narrator Johannes Climacus, Kierkegaard provides a reading of the *akedah* that highlights the moral significance of Abraham's action, showing how an incomprehensible passion leads Abraham up the mountain to kill his son. This situation must have been troubling for Isaac, at least, and Kierkegaard beautifully reworks the story to highlight concerns about the son. In one of his variations of the story, Abraham resolves not to conceal the truth from Isaac, and for a while maintains a sweet fatherly disposition. He was faced with a son who could not understand him. Kierkegaard writes:

> Then he turned away from Isaac for a moment, but when Isaac saw his face a second time it was changed, his gaze was wild, his mien one of horror. He caught Isaac by the chest, threw him to the ground and said: "Foolish boy, do you believe I am your father? I am an idolater. Do you believe this is God's command? No, it is my own desire." Then Isaac trembled and in his anguish cried: "God in heaven have mercy on me; if I have no father on earth, then be Thou my father!" But below his breath Abraham said to himself: "Lord in heaven I thank Thee; it is after all better that he believe I am a monster than that he lose faith in Thee."[22]

Abraham places responsibility on himself rather than risk having Isaac die in despair by believing God is unjust. A rebel against God is understandable; a God who demands a sacrificed son is not. Abraham has to make two impossibly difficult choices: first, he has to decide if the voice is God—and not insanity or the devil—and then has to choose whether to follow the command even if it is from God. In Kierkegaard's story, this

---

22. Kierkegaard, *Fear*, 45–46.

uncertainty leads to a crisis, and although he moves to kill the son, he sacrifices morality.

In this situation, responsibility falls upon Abraham as strongly as it does on Sethe. "In freedom," says Susanne Juhasz, "Sethe's maternal identification with her children develops to include both passion and responsibility"[23] and the same responsibility should apply to Abraham. God's command to Abraham violates both particular and universal morality. It is a personal and particular tragedy, since God takes away the son who God said would be given to Abraham. What's more, Isaac's death, according to that same promise, also destroys the future of the Jewish nation. Kierkegaard says that "in so far as the universal was there at all it was latent in Isaac, concealed as it were in his loins, and it would have to cry out with Isaac's mouth: 'Don't do it, you are destroying everything.'"[24] Similarly, Sethe is not only committing a transgression against the particular lives of the children, she is also harming the African American community by reinforcing stereotypes. In short, she kills what Morrison has set up to be the symbolic expression of the new, free, and self-possessed nation. Her family was, in her case as much as that of Abraham, the product of her body, but concealed deeper in the loins.

In his analysis of the *akedah,* Jerome Gellman says that most interpreters have failed to adequately imagine Abraham's torment. For many rabbis, in fact, the belief was that Abraham emotionally detached himself from his son, to the point where Gellman is prompted to exclaim that "for the early Hasidim, had Abraham felt love or pity for Isaac at the *akedah,* Abraham would have failed the test, even if he had sacrificed Isaac!"[25] Kierkegaard, on the other hand, draws attention to Abraham's anguish, as well as that of Isaac. *Fear and Trembling* begins with a section called an Attunement. Each section of the Attunement tries out an interpretation of the story, with this one, the third, being the most emotionally intense:

> It was early morning. Abraham rose in good time, kissed Sarah the young mother, and Sarah kissed Isaac, her delight, her joy for ever. And Abraham rode thoughtfully on. He thought of Hagar and of the son whom he had driven out into the desert. He climbed the mountain in Moriah, he drew the knife.

23. Juhasz, *Desire,* 115.
24. Kierkegaard, *Fear,* 88.
25. Gellman, *Abraham!,* 3.

> It was a tranquil evening when Abraham rode out alone, and he rode to the mountain in Moriah; he threw himself on his face, he begged God to forgive his sin at having been willing to sacrifice Isaac, at the father's having forgotten his duty to his son. He rode more frequently on his lonely way, but found no peace. He could not comprehend that it was a sin to have been willing to sacrifice to God *the best he owned*; that for which he would many times have gladly laid down his own life; and if it was a sin, if he had not so loved Isaac, then he could not understand that it could be forgiven; for what sin was more terrible?[26]

The sin here does not just affect Abraham and the future Jewish community; it affects Sarah as well. After all, it is not just *his* legacy that is at stake, but rather *her* emotional survival, if not a legacy of her own. Kierkegaard notes that, before the journey, "Sarah kissed Isaac, her delight, her joy for ever,"[27] which suggests that maternal immortality was at stake as much as paternal immortality. The biblical reference to the child as "the best" shows up near the end of *Beloved*, when Sethe laments to Paul D: "She was my best thing."[28]

While Kierkegaard's reading of the story is sensitive to interpersonal concerns, it also maintains traditional male impersonality. Kierkegaard notes that "Isaac told no one what he had seen."[29]ABraham keeps the traumatic experience to himself, and Gellman notes that a sense of "severe atomic selfhood" runs through Kierkegaard's understanding of the story, in which "an individual stands before the face of God alone, in transcendence of the horizontal plane of shared humanity." Feminist object relations theory, as he notes, is critical of the atomistic approach. Explaining the theory as it relates to gender identity, Gellman says that the original force in a child's life is the mother, whom "a boy must establish a 'separation from'" that results in "a desire for an atomic selfhood freed from the original setting of close identification with the mother."[30] A girl would not experience such a stark separation, since she can ease into autonomous selfhood by identification with the maternal role. There appears, however, to be little ease in Sethe's development, and *Beloved*, says Grewal, mourns "the breakup of the

---

26. Kierkegaard, *Fear*, 46.
27. Kierkegaard, *Fear*, 46–47, emphasis added.
28. Morrison, *Beloved*, 272.
29. Morrison, *Beloved*, 48.
30. Gellman, *Abraham!*, 91–92.

mother-daughter dyad, pried and swept asunder by the nightmare swirl of history . . . on to the shores of the living."[31]

If it were true that men must have an abrupt break from the maternal, while women can maintain contact, communication, and thus understanding with the maternal, *Beloved* shows that this contact is not always easy, but rather can take the form of a ghost that demands communication take place. Abraham and Isaac can keep the tragedy to themselves rather than express it through conversation and communion with others. Such communion is simply assumed by the narrator of *Beloved*. There is no room for autonomous selfhood at 124 Bluestone.

SETHE'S EXPRESSION

Beloved provides us with an alternative reading of Genesis 22. In *Beloved*'s most significant scene we see both similarities to the traditional understanding of the *akedah*, and yet important departures from it. These departures suggest an attempt by Morrison, among other things, to create a more woman-focused understanding of morality. To better understand the contrast, one can look at the first Attunement from *Fear and Trembling*, which ends with the following reverie:

> When the child is to be weaned the mother blackens her breast, for it would be a shame were the breast to look pleasing when the child is not to have it. So the child believes the breast has changed but the mother is the same, her look loving and tender as ever. Lucky the one that needed no more terrible means to wean the child![32]

Kierkegaard's example implies that mother-identification is primary. Abraham's trip up the mountain is a case of self-definition, but this self-definition is seen to be enacted, according to feminist object relations theory, as a reaction to the primacy of mother identification. The man must wean himself from the mother by identifying with something transcendent. In the case of Abraham, identification is with the Father. In the case of Kierkegaard's Isaac, the father fails and an imaginary Father takes over.

Morrison, however, brings Sethe's act of self-definition down to earth, and places it in a dirty barn surrounded by members of her community.

---

31. Grewal, "Memory," 142.
32. Kierkegaard, *Fear*, 47.

Here again the narrator provides shocking descriptions. After the sheriff leaves to get a cart, Baby Suggs, Sethe's mother-in-law and the spiritual leader of her community, tries desperately to reestablish a routine.

> "It's time you nurse the youngest," she said.
> Sethe reached up for the baby without letting the dead one go.
> Baby Suggs shook her head. "One at a time," she said and traded the living for the dead, which she carried into the keeping room. When she came back, Sethe was aiming a bloody nipple into the baby's mouth. Baby Suggs slammed her fist on the table and shouted, "Clean up! Clean yourself up!"
> They fought then. Like rivals over the heart of the loved, they fought. Each struggling for the nursing child. Baby Suggs lost when she slipped in a red puddle and fell. So Denver took her mother's milk right along with the blood of her sister.[33]

The women wrestle for the baby in the blood-soaked arena, creating an uncomfortably humorous ending to the scene. Perhaps most disturbing is the fact that Denver drinks a combination of blood and milk, creating an abomination of death and nourishment. The narrator describes it in a way that either suggests understatement or gossiping interest, and it is apparent that to some extent even the voice of the community has distanced itself out of psychological necessity. The lack of appropriate voice for trauma is of course a common theme in *Beloved*. Florian Bast ties this voicelessness specifically to the novel's use of the color red. "The infanticide she commits as a reaction," he says, reinforcing to some extent the animalistic interpretation of Sethe, "causes a trauma so fundamental to her psyche" that "Sethe, and thus the novel, cannot help but keep circling back to it in a perfect definition of compulsive repetition."[34]

The women's back-and-forth struggle for the baby is itself a sign of repetition of trauma, with no one willing to give in to move along the processing of the experience. The battle is over maternal propriety, if not also maternal property, and the situation is complicated further by the fact that Sethe's biological mother is nearly unknown to her. The mother-substitute, Baby Suggs, is indeed alive, although she has been psychologically wounded, particularly regarding the value of motherhood. She is reported to have discarded the children conceived from numerous rapes by White men. Sethe thus has an imperfect maternal role model. Stephanie Demetrakopoulos

---

33. Morrison, *Beloved*, 152.
34. Bast, "Red", 1076.

sees Sethe as an example of "women who have not had the opportunity to see the very flawed mothering of other women" self-imposing "impossible ideals of what good mothering is."[35] And as Angelyn Mitchell notes, Morrison "brilliantly complicates" the "nuanced properties of constructions like motherhood," ones that involve an interplay between self-centered and child-centered duties.[36] The former are exemplified in Suggs's older generation, while the latter are exemplified in Sethe, who arranged for her kids to escape, who travelled north while in late pregnancy, and who cared for children after she arrived.

Sethe was free for twenty-eight days, and as Medoro notices, this is one full moon and menstrual cycle. Accordingly, "the murder she commits becomes a kind of regenerative bleeding,"[37] a sign of her defiance of patriarchy, slavery, and motherhood in that context. For psychologist Ginette Paris, the Judeo-Christian aversion to this kind of bloodshed is clearly defensive, since in pagan cultures, "far from being seen as an evil substance, it was considered to be endowed with magical powers." Following this, one would be likely to see Sethe not just as the proto-Egyptian Seth, but also as the Greek goddess Artemis, a god who "offers both protection and death to women, children, and animals."[38] "As with slavery," Paris says, "one person controls the body of another and prevents normal relationships from developing with others and with the child. The unwanted child, like the children of slaves, carries the brand of domination even before coming into the world."[39]

Sethe's rebellion against the brand of domination has a precedent. Although Baby Suggs admonishes Sethe for her bloody uncleanliness in the barn, she also might on a deeper level sympathize with Sethe's defiance. Sethe is thus still bound by a maternal history that showed infanticide as an option, and seems to be following directives of maternal duty when she decides to kill her children rather than have them owned. Nonetheless, Abraham's Father is arguably a worse parental figure than Sethe, since, in his divine privilege, he requires filicide apparently for no reason other than that of jealously owning Abraham's will. At least Sethe was not administering a test but was deadly serious.

35. Demetrakopoulos, "Bonds," 56.
36. Mitchell, *Freedom*, 98.
37. Medoro, *Bleeding*, 165.
38. Paris, *Psychology*, 5.
39. Paris, *Psychology*, 47.

As she wields the blade, Sethe is bound by mysterious imperatives from traditional mothers; as Abraham wields the blade, he is guided by mysterious imperatives from a transcendent Father. In the words of Andrea O'Reilly, "what Sethe claims is not necessarily ownership but a biological, emotional mother-child bond, which for her has primacy and authority over the law of the Father."[40] All of this occurs, O'Reilly says, because of a "murdered baby girl" and "a symbolic representation of the broken motherline—the 'sixty million and more' to whom the book is dedicated."[41] The "sixty million" reference has prompted discussion of Morrison's intentions in including it. Is it a one-upping of the six million Jews believed to have died in the Holocaust? Naomi Mandel argues that the dedication is not to be taken as invoking a quantitative comparison of atrocities against Africans and Jews, but constitutes "a vague approximation that serves the purpose of evoking a vast array of dead bodies rather than counting and accounting for the bodies themselves."[42] In doing so, however, it risks making death into a mass noun rather than a count noun—a philosophically interesting move, but one which can lead to historical *discounting* of evils. Nonetheless, the point here should not be that of noting quantity, but rather gendered qualities. Sethe was allowed to break her motherline, while Abraham was saved from breaking his fatherline.

ANGELIC INTERVENTION

The angel restrains Abraham. According to the midrash, the angel had to call Abraham's name twice, because he was so intent on killing.[43] Fortunately, though, the murder is averted, and (problematic in its own way) the animal substitution takes place. The traditional understanding of the story lauds Abraham as being extraordinarily faithful. Sethe is not so lucky. Although Stamp Paid saves her from killing Denver, he does not save her from killing the baby. Sethe is alone in the scene because her family and friends were silent about the approach of the reclamation team. Her community is similar to the servants who attended Abraham on his journey, but who left as he approached the mountaintop. Sethe remains at ground

---

40. O'Reilly, *Motherhood*, 136.
41. O'Reilly, *Motherhood*, 86.
42. Mandel, *Unspeakable*, 170.
43. Gellman, *Abraham!*, 99.

level, experiencing loneliness and atomic selfhood not through her own lofty movements, but through a betrayal by others.

Sethe's story is not one of honor and prosperity. She maintains a humble home life with Denver and has to deal with Beloved haunting the house. When Paul D arrives, the relationship they start is strained by the presence of a fully embodied ghost, one that apparently seduces Paul D. Denver harbors a jealousy for the mysterious woman, whose connection to Sethe is deep and destructive. Paul D becomes one of the many who fail to understand her, while the community in general maintains its distance from the house.

Her story does, however, have a scene of redemption. The neighborhood women congregate in front of 124 Bluestone in order to exorcise the ghost. Describing this scene, the narrator notes that "in the beginning there were no words. In the beginning was the sound . . ."[44] This allusion to the Gospel of John allows Morrison to contrast the word, the *logos*, with the primal affect of a singing or moaning sound. As Hannes Bergthaller notes, "Morrison's wording explicitly sets it into a Western (more specifically, a Judeo-Christian) understanding of language" that is "closer to music" and which "communicates no particular meanings but only the togetherness of the community."[45] She subverts the traditional masculine emphasis on language and rational discourse with a prerational affect exemplified in the first coos and cries of a child to its mother, and any community assembled to watch. In the midst of this original emotion arrives the figure of Edward Bodwin, a White man known for defending former slaves like Sethe. In this case, he is there to help Denver, who had been freeing herself from the seclusion of her mother's haunted home. Sethe was outside the house, breaking ice with a pick, when the sight of Bodwin elicits the traumatic memory of the bloody barn. Her thoughts are that

> He is coming into her yard and he is coming for her best thing. She hears wings. Little hummingbirds stick needle beaks right through her headcloth into her hair and beat their wings. And if she thinks anything it is no. No no. Nonono. She flies. The ice pick is not in her hand; it is her hand.[46]

The image Morrison creates here is similar to paintings whose subject is the *akedah*. In Titian's *Abraham and Isaac*, for example, Abraham's

---

44. Morrison, *Beloved*, 259.
45. Bergthaller, "Dis(re)membering," 132.
46. Morrison, *Beloved*, 262.

knife-arm is raised over his son, muscles tensed in conformity with the single-minded will to kill. Bodwin is the Isaac of the scene, experiencing something beyond his control and understanding. And Sethe is Abraham, acting against both self-interest, and the interests of those around her, because, as Furman notes, Bodwin's murder would have "endangered the entire black community."[47] His death would be the end of White benevolence; similarly, the death of Isaac would mean the end of the Jewish people, whom God said would live through Abraham's son.

If Sethe's behavior perplexes Bodwin, this is largely because despite his general sympathetic nature he is still White and privileged. He looks on as Sethe is intercepted by Denver, who, along with another member of the former slave community, restrains Sethe's arm. These women become Sethe's angels. Abraham has his fair-skinned angel, braced with heavenly power. Sethe, on the other hand, has a "hill of black people, falling" around her.[48] It is the community that saves Sethe and restrains her will. Yet even though the community saves her from being a murderer in this new situation, it still does not understand her. Paul D and Stamp Paid later discuss the event with a "seriousness and embarrassment" that "made them shake with laughter."[49]

If we consider Abraham a hero for being willing to sacrifice his son to a mysterious directive from God, one that defies moral reasoning, Sethe should also be considered a hero for being willing to sacrifice her daughter to a less mysterious directive, one in opposition to the evil of slavery. Her belief is that slavery is so bad that it warrants such a decision. It is an understanding that

> anyone white could take your whole self for anything that came to mind. Not just work, kill, or maim you, but dirty you. Dirty you so bad you couldn't like yourself anymore. . . . The best thing she was, was her children. White may dirty *her* all right, but not her best thing . . .[50]

Sethe is not so easily regarded as a hero, which suggests that we do not have an idea of maternal heroism to match the paternal heroism traditionally attributed to Abraham. Either that, or we should consider both Sethe and Abraham to be of questionable moral character. Yet if Sethe is just an

---

47. Furman, "Re-memories," 269.
48. Morrison, *Beloved*, 262.
49. Morrison, *Beloved*, 265.
50. Morrison, *Beloved*, 251.

instinctive animal, then Abraham is a moral monster. He kills because he follows the sacrificial mania of a morally remote God; she kills out of her own sense of mercy.

7

JOHN BROWN, BRING HIM DOWN

A late 1980s American rock band named Masters of Reality made just a small contribution toward changing music or popular culture. I would like to believe this was because of accidents of promotional interest in the music industry, not because of lack of personal inspiration. Perhaps its obscurity should not be attributed to an indifferent music industry, but rather to the fact that, like a prophet, their message was not understood at the time. One of the band's songs from the band's 1988 self-titled album was called "John Brown," in which singer/songwriter Chris Goss created the following lyrics:

> John Brown, bring him down
> Pull his body to the ground.
> Left him up for long enough,
> Let me be the baby gruff.
> Holiday, holiday
> We pull John Brown at noon today
> Tomorrow Day, nothing rings
> Nothing rings and nothing brings.

Here we have references to John Brown's hanged body, and the call for an anti-holiday of silence. The last two lines, presented in the poetically repetitive form also used in Old Testament poetry, indicate the end of sacrifice. All of this is sung along with heroic folk song accompaniment, inspired by the edgy Civil War anthem "John Brown's Body." This song, justifying the Union army, was later smoothed out into the "Battle Hymn of the Republic."

One variation on this folk tradition calls John Brown a "John the Baptist of the Christ we are to see," and says that Brown looks down from heaven at "the conflict that he heralded" and especially "on the army of the Union with its flag red, white, and blue." This quasi-religious use of the American flag is relatively new in United States history. Theologian Harry Stout notes that the American flag only became a common symbol of patriotism during the Civil War, before which it was found mostly for identification on ships.[1] The war vivified its blood-red stripes in the American Imaginary.

The Civil War was, and continues to be, rich with symbolism. Theologian Horace Bushnell argued soon after the war that this event was a vicarious atonement for America's sins, "quite literally a blood sacrifice required by God for sinners North and South."[2] This metaphorical combination of body and battlefield suggests a peculiar form of Christianity that to a prophetic pragmatist like Cornel West would be idolatrous. And anti-war theologian Stanley Hauerwas says that "if the Civil War teaches us anything, it makes clear what happens when Christians no longer believe that Christ's sacrifice is sufficient for the salvation of the world. As a result," he concludes, "Christians confuse the sacrifice of war with the sacrifice of Christ."[3]

This confusion is so apparent for Bushnell, who despite his notoriety for critiquing the penal substitutionary theory of the atonement, nonetheless is caught up in the idea of violent sacrifice. He says that "we do not commonly speak of those who give up their lives on the battle-fields of their country as dying by martyrdom. And yet it is the martyrdom of loyalty into which they freely gave their bodies and knowingly consented to the sacrifice." He believed that "according to the true economy of the world, so many of its grandest and most noble benefits have and are to have a tragic origin, and to come only as outgrowths of blood."[4] Biographer Robert Bruce Mullin's summary of Bushnell's views shows the extent to which the pastor was caught up in the nationalist idolatry: "The law of God taught that only through the shedding of blood could greatness be accomplished.... Through the blood shed in the war a new chapter had

---

1. Quoted in Carson and Ebel, *Jeremiad*, 224.
2. Quoted in Carson and Ebel, *Jeremiad*, 226.
3. Quoted in Carson and Ebel, *Jeremiad*, 229.
4. Quoted in Mullin, *Puritan as Yankee*, 116.

opened up for the nation. Before the great carnage the various states had simply been 'kenneled under the Constitution and not reconciled,' but now a unity had been cemented, one much deeper than that of the law." Bushnell himself, in an essay that Mullin describes as "one of the most moving and one of the most troubling of Bushnell's works," describes how Black people were also to be included in the sacrificial piety, and recalls with loving admiration "the bloody fight and victory on the James, where the ground itself was black with dead."[5]

This reference to a bloody fight would not be out of place within the fringes of abortion rights discourse today. The most compelling defenses of abortion rights refer to the effects of abortion prohibition on women of color especially. The image of the back-alley abortion tragedy lends itself to a sacralization of the bodies, usually imagined as Black and brown, as sacrifices in a fight against oppression. One more imaginative move, and the notorious dark and bloody figures of aborted fetuses also become part of the fight, and the floor of clinics is black with dead.

The 1988 version of the John Brown folk tradition suggests that it is time to end the sacrifices. Brown was hanged, not crucified, so the leader of "Bleeding Kansas" is, biblically speaking, an imperfect sacrifice anyway. Goss's "holiday" can thus be understood as a recognition of our freedom from the necessity of violent sacrifice. When performing the song, Goss would include the introductory line "Come on, children, gather 'round, and hear the story of old John Brown." This chilling call for innocent kids to hear the story of bodies, blood, and the Kansas battleground only makes moral sense if we interpret the song as proclaiming an end to sacrifice in future generations. The story should be about the removal of the body, not the veneration of it.

BODIES AND BATTLEFIELDS: SORTING THEM OUT

Admittedly, this book has taken the easier route of addressing the moral sentiments behind policy rather than the policy itself. Policy is based on the sentiments, where reasons are deployed as moves for domination. It is similar to the board game Risk, in which players strategize in order to take over territories. Yet we can propose an important change. Instead of merely rolling the dice to determine victory or defeat, the players must also construct a justification for the war, which they present to their people.

---

5. Quoted in Carson and Ebel, *Jeremiad*, 224–25.

They then roll the dice to determine if the people believe their justification. And just like in the ordinary game, where victories garner greater military resources, in the new game, every war creates either new sentiments of violence or sentiments of revolution within the people.

It is our goal to promote the revolution of sentiments and do this through, among other things, philosophizing. As William James says in his lectures on *Pragmatism*,

> The history of philosophy is to a great extent that of a certain clash of human temperaments. Undignified as such a treatment may seem to some of my colleagues, I shall have to take account of this clash and explain a good many of the divergencies of philosophers by it. Of whatever temperament a professional philosopher is, he tries when philosophizing to sink the fact of his temperament. Temperament is no conventionally recognized reason, so he urges impersonal reasons only for his conclusions. Yet his temperament really gives him a stronger bias than any of his more strictly objective premises.[6]

In saying that temperament is behind all philosophy, James does not mean that we should have blind allegiance to temperament. James merely wants us to acknowledge that this allegiance is what motivates us to provide reasons. Yet there is a symbiotic relationship, and impersonal reasons can work their way down to the temperamental depths. The temperamental depths, thus altered, in turn alter the reasons that are given. Like a river, though, the currents above move faster than those below. Currents flow, while sentiments change slowly.

Philosophy is a competition of individual tastes *modified* through reasons. Clashes of temperament, it is hoped, remain nonviolent. We are attacking the others' temperaments instead of their bodies. The advantage of this approach is that there does not have to be clear winners and losers. The practical reality of war is that, despite any superficial assignment of victory to one side, in the war itself there is little beyond abstract nationalism that differentiates the nations. The result of the conflict is sacrificed bodies, usually along with some change in moral sentiments among the people. Because of this Bushnell can talk about sacrificed bodies as a reflection of a deep change in US culture, a change as deep as that believed by Christians to result from the death of Christ. My sentiments go deeper though, and they refuse to assent to Bushnell's determinism and his need to interpret

---

6. James, *Pragmatism*, 11.

the sacrifices of soldiers as the result of some willed nobleness, rather than the result of a collective will inscribing itself on the bodies of soldiers, themselves inscribing a blood sacrifice onto the battlefields. Christ is the only willing sacrifice, because only a Christ is able to stand outside of the deception that makes humans mythologize war into a sacred possession.

Our prophetic pragmatism concludes that war and abortion are symptoms of the same disease, and this disease is not treated well when we merely create a sacrificial piety that distracts us from the need to make hard choices, choices as hard as those of Sethe in the barnyard. This prophetic pragmatism must also at least give some indication of how to begin changing the moral sentiments. As satisfying as it is to talk literarily about Sisyphean tasks—even the kind that Paglia seems to recommend in her feminist battle against nature—it remains that if there is a possibility of escape from the fate of continually killing and continually opposing those who kill, the possibility should be pursued. One question to ask is whether, due to some kind of political necessity, one would have to choose which of the two evils to address first—war or abortion.

When I step outside of moral sentiments into the relatively disingenuous word of reasons, I have an obvious bias toward ending war. Violence, I believe, works from the outside in. State violence works its way into the body, and the State cannot protect anything except through violence, explicit or implicit. The origin of violence is collective action with individual choice as a derivative. If we consider the matter as one of entailment, we have the collective violence of war and scapegoating as the larger of the circles, with abortion within. Anthropologically, war preceded voluntary abortion, and what's more, voluntary abortion is a recent practice within a much longer history of involuntary abortion. It is thus appropriate, I believe, to see abortion as the result of war, and thus implicate men more than women, and consequently approach the topic as was done in chapter 1, namely by avoiding legal inscriptions on the bodies of women and promoting changes in our moral sentiments. As we move away from violence and sacrifice, we move away from the control of bodies and the sacralization of battlefields. The problem is that changing sentiments is a slower process than changing laws. The United States war machine is unprecedented in world history, and its effects on the sentiments of Americans, if not the world, is also unprecedented. Changing the culture of war will require avoiding some common mistakes. Following the work of anthropologist Douglas Fry, philosopher David Swanson says that wars are not driven by an everpresent minority of sociopaths or avoided by controlling them. Wars are not made inevitable by resource scarcity or inequality or prevented by prosperity and shared wealth. Wars are not determined by the weaponry available of the influence of the profiteers. All such factors play parts in wars, but none of them can make wars *inevitable*.

Swanson continues by saying that

> The decisive factor is a militaristic culture, a culture that glorifies war or even just accepts it (and you can accept something even while telling a pollster you oppose it; real opposition takes work). War spreads as other memes spread, culturally. The abolition of war can do the same.[7]

One can substitute the word *abortions* for *wars* in the first quote and understand one of the principle points of this book. The inevitability factor is what I am referring to as the tragic element, itself part of the idea of *sacrifice*. And if we can sacrifice full-grown people in war rather than fix a political problem, how much easier is it to sacrifice fetuses rather than fix a social problem?

The only thing that can be critiqued here is Swanson's deterministic comment that opposition to war requires work. The person who merely indicates an anti-war choice to a pollster, and does little more, is neither hypocritical nor lazy. They are acting in the way that we all should act. We should not have to work against a moral evil.

What's more, activism *against* war is ultimately a losing battle. The metaphors of war are legion: the war against nature, the war against drugs, the war against crime, the war against cancer, the war against COVID-19. When we speak of battles we are adopting the language of war. We are trying of course to sublimate the war sentiments, but this process of sublimation continues to preserve the war sentiment, in the same way that a flywheel preserves the motion of a machine. The real thing is always ready to step in. In the novel *End Zone*, the professor had it mostly right: football is not a metaphor for war, since it is functioning to preserve war and the sentiments associated with it.

These sentiments motivate the arguments such that, in discussions of war, the pacifist is often made to answer the questions, such as when they would accept the legitimacy of violence. And thus the pacifist has lost from the start, since the debate takes place on the war apologists' territory. In

7. Swanson, *Abolition*, 67.

a lecture titled "The Moral Equivalent of War," James says that "'peace' in military mouths today, is a synonym for 'war expected.'" James continues by saying, hyperbolically, that

> the word has become a pure provocative, and no government wishing peace sincerely should allow it ever to be printed in a newspaper. Every up-to-date dictionary should say that "peace" and "war" mean the same thing, now *in posse*, now *in actu*. It may even reasonably be said that the intensely sharp *preparation* for war by the nations is the *real war*, permanent, unceasing; and that the battles are only a sort of public verification of the mastery gained during the "peace"-interval.[8]

James's answer is to work with the war sentiments, and create social service conscription in a war on Nature. The failure of such a vision is apparent when considering that we have already destroyed nature, and now humanity is much like Ehrenreich's post-prey male looking for something to do with his life. What's more, James is correct (even if hyperbolic) in saying that we should avoid the word *peace*, but he would be better to say that we should avoid the word *battles*. Promoting the War on Nature, or any war, might seem like a "pragmatic" compromise, but in the long term it serves the purposes of war the way that the NFL does, by inflaming war sentiments in a safer setting, but knowing that the smoldering can be inflamed at any moment when the possibility of real war presents itself.

A BURIAL

In the century and a half since Emerson engaged the topic of rivalry and violence, Christianity in the United States has progressed to the point where it would not be surprising to see an image of Jesus on the cross, and two American soldiers crucified on either side. At one time, these would have been Union and Confederate soldiers. Today, there would be one who believes in the cult of blood sacrifice, affirming the sacrifice for freedom, and another who does not. Jesus would be blessing only the believer in sacrifice.

It is time to bring all of the bodies to the ground. The development of this body-sacrificial American religion is signified in both Ralph Waldo Emerson and John Brown. Speaking after Brown's arrest for raiding Harper's Ferry to arm the abolitionists, Emerson extols Brown's "simple, artless

---

8. James, *Heart*, 301–13.

goodness." He notes that Brown helped his farmer father provide for the army in the War of 1812. Emerson says that "gentlemen find traits of relation readily between him and themselves" and that with Brown there is an "innocent pleading, as of childhood!" Brown's execution is the "*reductio ad aburdum* of Slavery, when the Governor of Virginia is forced to hang a man whom he declares to be a man of the most integrity, truthfulness and courage."[9] And yet another *reductio* occurs when we consider a God who would send to death a Son considered the most unworthy of death.

A year after Brown was hanged, Emerson gave another speech, relating the story of how Brown befriended a Black slave while collecting cattle, and later saw this man beaten with an iron shovel. This "worked such an indignation in him that he swore an oath of resistance to Slavery as long as he lived." Every blow to his Black friend's body was a strike that drew Brown to understand the depth of his moral sentiment regarding violence and sacrifice. Emerson notes that he sides with Brown's statement that his dedication to ending slavery was not just the result of a boyhood oath, but "was all settled millions of years before the world was made."[10] There are two ways of viewing this line. On one, Brown is referring to freedom from bondage as being the original divine imperative, while on the other he is referring, in his unconscious childhood frankness, to violent sacrifice being the primordial sin. Brown's final words, written to a guard prior to his hanging, were:

> I, John Brown, am now quite certain that the crimes of this guilty land can never be purged away but with blood.[11]

Emerson's line that John Brown "will make the gallows holy as the cross," is prophetic much in the way that WBC is prophetic. For in Emerson's sacralizing of the violence, a violence done both by the body John Brown and to the body of John Brown, we disclose the sacrificial thinking whose trajectory extends to the present.

A PRAYER

Emerson said of prayer:

---

9. Emerson, *Writings*, 796.
10. Emerson, *Works*.
11. Quoted in Hinton, *John Brown*, 398.

> Prayer that craves a particular commodity—anything less than all good, is vicious. Prayer is the contemplation of the facts of life from the highest point of view. It is the soliloquy of a beholding and jubilant soul. It is the spirit of God pronouncing his works good. But prayer as a means to effect a private end is meanness and theft. It supposes dualism and not unity in nature and consciousness. As soon as the man is at one with God, he will not beg.[12]

It's not always easy for philosophers to find their off button, and so when I hear someone asking for thoughts and prayers toward a certain person with a certain problem, I feel compelled to consider the matter philosophically. The problem that the specific person is experiencing is bad, but there are other people experiencing the same problem, and so why should this person's problem get special attention, just by virtue of being promulgated by some other person whom I happen to know? If one person's problem just happens to be the one brought to my attention, that does not make it in itself more attention-worthy than a stranger who manifests that same problem. So then it seems better that I should pray for all people experiencing that problem, but then another question comes up: What makes these problems generally more worthy of attention than other problems? If, for example, two people are both suffering from cancer, I can pray for both, and then pray for all who have cancer, but why then is cancer more important than other diseases? If we pray for an end to all diseases, what makes disease more important than, for example, the violence of war? Cancer might be less curable that war, but that is not really the point. The fact that it is less curable could mean either that prayers are relatively useless, since there is little left for us to do; or it could mean that prayers are especially needed, since because there is little for us to do, we need to rely on God to do it. A similar situation occurs with war. Praying to end war might motivate us to stop it, or it might make us believe that war is unstoppable except by appeal to a higher power.

The synthesis of determinism and choice is tragedy, and with both war and abortion the final appeal usually ends with a call, no more efficacious than an Emerson prayer, for some kind of mourning. The words of James Gustafson, teacher of the anti-war theologian Stanley Hauerwas, disclose much about moral sentiments in American culture:

> As the morally conscientious soldier fighting in a particular war is convinced that life can and ought to be taken, "justly" but also

---

12. Emerson, *Writings*, 147–48.

"mournfully," so the moralists can be convinced that the defenseless fetus can be taken, less justly but more mournfully.[13]

Ending with mourning resigns us to tragedy and sacrifice. We mourn premature deaths because we believe that person's life should have been extended, and we mourn mature deaths because we believe life itself should be extended. To mourn either abortion or war is to mistake the human unwillingness to change itself for an inhuman limiting force on change. This mistake is based on seeing ourselves as being in the midst of something thrust upon us from some inhuman reality, rather than seeing ourselves as in the midst of something of our own creation. Literary theorist Rene Girard notes that "we have yet to learn how man succeeds in positing his own violence as an independent being."[14] One way men do this, however, is to discharge violence onto other bodies. In war this is most apparent, when bodies are killed out in the open. But as we look further, we see this violence finding its way into the act of abortion, which does not arise from a world of extrahuman necessity, but is the result of a failure shared by all, and falsely sanctified through individual choice. Dorothy Day, whose somber sentiments began this exploration of abortion and war, is to be taken seriously. A child's existence does not depend on national war-violence that clears the way for its existence. On the contrary, *Bodies and Battlefields* has argued that it is this context of national war-violence that conditions the choice of abortion. If violence seems to solve problems in the world, it also seems like it might solve problems within bodies. As shown in the characters of Ellen Bezukhov, Ruth Stoops, and Sethe—and in the real-life case of the women in the Chicago Shakedown—our anxieties can be awkwardly focused on the bodies of women, with tragic results. Instead of starting with the bodies, I suggest we start with the world. Instead of addressing problems from the inside out, we address them from the outside in. Instead of individual sacrifice, profound social change.

Whether the choice of abortion is to remain a legal option remains beyond the interest of our investigation. In some ways the question is similar to that of war. Outlawing war seems to make us feel that we are doing something, but it is more the violence involved in enforcing laws, and not the laws themselves, that stops the actions. This is to say in effect that war is what stops war. And a similar pointless war need not take place in the case of abortion. We have indeed made our bodies into battlefields, and it is time

13. Gustafson, in Bainton, *Attitudes*, 89.
14. Girard, *Violence*, 30.

to reject all moral sentiments that make this seem like we are participating in some kind of a sacred obligation, that is, something believed to be beyond our control.

BIBLIOGRAPHY

Addams, Jane. *A Centennial Reader*. New York: MacMillan, 1960.
———. *Newer Ideals of Peace*. Chicago: University of Illinois Press, 2007.
———. *Peace and Bread in Times of War*. Chicago: University of Illinois Press, 2002.
Alexandre, Sandy. "From the Same Tree: Gender and Iconography in Representations of Violence in *Beloved*." *Signs* 36:4 (2001) 915–40.
Arner, Rob. *Consistently Pro-Life: The Ethics of Bloodshed in Ancient Christianity*. Eugene, OR: Pickwick, 2010.
Associated Press. "High Court: Does Father's Pain Trump Free Speech?" October 6, 2010. http://www.rickross.com/reference/westboro/westboro111.html.
Bainton, Roland H. *Christian Attitudes toward War and Peace*. New York: Abingdon, 1960.
Bast, Florian. "Reading Red: The Troping of Trauma in Toni Morrison's *Beloved*." *Callaloo* 34:4 (2011) 1069–86.
Bergthaller, Hannes. "Dis(re)membering History's *revenants*: Trauma, Writing, and Simulated Orality in Toni Morrison's *Beloved*." *Connotations* 16:1–3 (2006/2007) 116–36.
Bushman, Richard, ed. *The Great Awakening: Documents on the Revival of Religion, 1740–1745*. Kingsport, TN: Kingsport, 1969.
Byrd, Charles Michael (Charukrishna). *The Bhagavad Gita in Black and White. From Mulatto Pride to Krishna Consciousness*. Palm Coast, FL: Backintyme, 2007.
Campbell, James. *Recovering Benjamin Franklin*. Chicago: Open Court, 1999.
Carson, John D., and Jonathan H. Ebel. *From Jeremiad to Jihad: Religion, Violence and America*. Berkeley, CA: University of California Press, 2012.
CNN. "Counterprotestors Confront Westboro Baptist Church at Arlington." May 31, 2011. <http://www.cnn.com/2011/US/05/30/arlington.cemetery.protesters/index.html>.
Cobb, Michael. *God Hates Fags: The Rhetorics of Religious Violence*. New York: New York University Press, 2006.
Darling, Marsha. "In the Realm of Responsibility: A Conversation with Toni Morrison." In *Conversations with Toni Morrison*, edited by Danille Taylor-Guthrie, 246–54. Jackson, MS: University of Mississippi Press, 1994.
Day, Dorothy. *Selected Writings*. Edited by Robert Ellsberg. New York: Orbis, 1983.
DeLillo, Don. *End Zone*. New York: Penguin, 1972.
Demetrakopoulos, Stephanie. "Maternal Bonds as Devourers of Women's Individuation in Toni Morrison's *Beloved*." *African American Review* 26:1 (1992) 51–59.

Dutton, Denis. *The Art Instinct: Beauty, Pleasure, and Human Evolution*. New York: Bloomsbury, 2009.
Eagleton, Terry. *The Meaning of Life*. New York: Oxford University Press, 2007.
Edwards, Jonathan. *The Nature of True Virtue*. Ann Arbor, MI: University of Michigan Press, 1960.
———. "Sinners in the Hands of an Angry God." In *Pragmatism and Religion: Classical Sources and Original Essays*, edited by Stuart Rosenbaum, 24–27. Urbana, IL: University of Chicago Press, 2003.
Ehrenreich, Barbara. *Blood Rites: Origins and History of the Passions of War*. New York: Henry Holt, 1997.
Emerson, Ralph Waldo. *Selected Writings*. New York: The Modern Library, 1992.
———. *Complete Works: Vol XI*. New York: Houghton, Mifflin, and Company, 1904.
Eno, Greg. "Former Detroit Lions Guard Mike Utley Determined to Do His Own 'Walk-Off.'" *Bleacher Report*. https://bleacherreport.com/articles/947333-former-detroit-lions-guard-mike-utley-determined-to-do-his-own-walk-off.
Furman, Jan. "Sethe's Re-memories: The Covert Return of What is Best Forgotten." In *Critical Essays on Toni Morrison's* Beloved, edited by Barbara H. Solomon, 261–71. New York: G. K. Hall, 1998.
Gellman, Jerome I. *Abraham! Abraham! Kierkegaard and the Hasidim on the Binding of Isaac*. Burlington, VT: Ashgate, 2003.
Girard, Rene. *Violence and the Sacred*. Baltimore: Johns Hopkins University Press, 1972.
Glaude, Eddie. *In a Shade of Blue: Pragmatism and the Politics of Black America*. Chicago: University of Chicago Press, 2007.
Goldberg, Bernard. *100 People Who Are Screwing Up America*. New York: HarperCollins, 2005.
Grewal, Gurleen. "Memory and the Matrix of History: The Poetics of Loss and Recovery in Joy Kogawa's *Obasan* and Toni Morrison's *Beloved*." In *Memory and Cultural Politics: New Approaches to American Ethnic Literatures*, edited by Amrijit Singh, Joseph T. Skerret Jr., and Robert F. Hoga, 140–74. Boston: Northeastern University Press, 1996.
Grosz, Elizabeth. *Space, Time, and Perversion: Essays on the Politics of Bodies*. New York: Routledge, 1994.
Hamner, M. Gail. *American Pragmatism: A Religious Genealogy*. New York: Oxford University Press, 2003.
Hedges, Chris. *War Is the Force That Gives Us Meaning*. New York: Random House, 2002.
Hinton, Richard J. *John Brown and His Men: With Some Account of the Roads They Traveled to Reach Harper's Ferry*. New York: Funk and Wagnalls, 1894.
Hirshman, Linda R. *Get to Work: A Manifesto for Women of the World*. New York: Viking, 2006.
Howe, Julia Ward. "Mother's Day Proclamation." In *Stop the Next War Now: Effective Responses to Violence and Terrorism*, edited by Medea Benjamin and Jodie Evans, 82–83. San Francisco: Inner Ocean, 2005.
James, William. *The Heart of William James*. Edited by Robert Richardson. Cambridge, MA: Harvard University Press, 2010.
———. *Pragmatism*. Cambridge, MA: Harvard University Press, 1975.
Juhasz, Suzanne. *A Desire for Women: Relational Psychoanalysis, Writing, and Relationships Between Women*. New Brunswick, NJ: Rutgers University Press, 2003.
Kierkegaard, Søren. *Fear and Trembling*. New York: Penguin, 1985.

Kirkemo, Ronald. *Between the Eagle and the Dove: The Christian and American Foreign Policy.* Downers Grove, IL: InterVarsity, 1976.

Kloeckner, Alfred J. "Intellect and Moral Sentiment in Emerson's Opinions of 'The Meaner Kinds' of Men." *American Literature* 30:3 (November 1958) 322–28.

Kodat, Catherine Gunther. "'Margaret Garner' and the Second Tear." *American Quarterly* 60:1 (2008) 159–71.

Kyung, Chung Hyun. *Struggle to be the Sun Again: Introducing Asian Women's Theology.* Maryknoll, NY: Orbis, 1990.

Laughing Baby. YouTube video, August 25, 2006. https://www.youtube.com/watch?v=HttF5HVYtlQ.

Madson, Joshua. "A Non-Violent Reading of the *Book of Mormon*." In *War & Peace in Our Time: Mormon Perspectives*, edited by Patrick Q. Mason, David Pulsipher, and Richard L. Bushman, 13–28. Salt Lake City: Greg Kofford, 2012.

Mandel, Naomi. *Against the Unspeakable: Complicity, the Holocaust, and Slavery.* Charlottesville, VA: University of Virginia Press, 2006.

Manninen, Bertha Alvarez. *Pro-Life, Pro-Choice: Shared Values in the Abortion Debate.* Nashville: Vanderbilt University Press, 2014.

Medoro, Dana. *The Bleeding of America: Menstruation as Symbolic Economy in Pynchon, Faulkner and Morrison.* Westport, CT: Greenwood, 2002.

Miller, Perry. "The Resolution of Nonconformity." In *Puritanism and the American Experience*, edited by Michael McGiffert, 142–53. Reading, MA: Addison-Wesley, 1969.

Mitchell, Angelyn. *The Freedom to Remember: Narrative, Slavery, and Gender in Contemporary Black Women's Fiction.* New Brunswick, NJ: Rutgers University Press, 2002.

Morgan, Edmund S. *The Puritan Dilemma: The Story of John Winthrop.* Boston: Little, Brown and Company, 1958.

Morrison, Toni. *Beloved.* New York: Plume, 1988.

Mullin, Robert Bruce. *The Puritan as Yankee: A Life of Horace Bushnell.* Grand Rapids: Eerdmans, 2002.

Oates, Joyce Carol. *On Boxing.* Hopewell, NJ: Ecco, 1994.

Onion, The. "U.S. out of My Uterus vs. We Must Deploy Troops to Jessica Linden's Uterus Immediately." September 22, 1999. https://www.theonion.com/u-s-out-of-my-uterus-vs-we-must-deploy-troops-to-jess-1819594277.

O'Reilly, Andrea. *Toni Morrison and Motherhood: A Politics of the Heart.* Albany, NY: State University of New York Press, 2004.

Otten, Terry. *The Crime of Innocence in the Fiction of Toni Morrison.* Columbia, MO: University of Missouri Press, 1989.

Paglia, Camille. *Sex, Art, and American Culture.* New York: Vintage, 1992.

———. *Vamps & Tramps.* New York: Vintage, 1994.

Paris, Ginette. *The Psychology of Abortion.* Putnam, CT.: Spring, 1992.

Payne, Alexander, dir. *Citizen Ruth.* Hollywood, CA: Miramax Films, 1996.

"Phelps Troop Hating." YouTube video, 2003. https://www.youtube.com/watch?v=ioDAkFZt5Vo.

Reagan, Leslie J. "'About to Meet Her Maker': Women, Doctors, Dying Declarations, and the State's Investigation of Abortion." *The Journal of American History* 77:4 (1991) 569–98.

Richardson, Robert D. *Emerson: The Mind on Fire*. Berkeley: University of California Press, 1995.

Rodrigues, Eusebio L. "The Telling of *Beloved*." *The Journal of Narrative Technique* 21:2 (1991) 1240–64.

Schadt, Devin. *Show Us the Father: 7 Secrets to be a Father on Earth Like the Father in Heaven*. Lakewood, CO: Totus Tuus, 2016.

Schneider, Herbert W. "Ungodly Puritans." In *Puritanism and the American Experience*, edited by Michael McGiffert, 142–54. Reading, MA: Addison-Wesley, 1969.

Scubla, Lucien. *Giving Life, Giving Death: Psychoanalysis, Anthropology, Philosophy*. Lansing, MI: Michigan State University Press, 2014.

Suckiel, Ellen Kappy. *Heaven's Champion: William James' Philosophy of Religion*. South Bend, IN: University of Notre Dame Press, 1998.

Singer, Margaret Thaler. *Cults in our Midst*. San Francisco: Jossey-Bass, 2003.

Stout, Harry S. "Review Essay: Religion, War, and the Meaning of America." *Religion and American Culture: A Journal of Interpretation* 19:2 (2009) 275–89. doi:10.1525/rac.2009.19.2.275.

Swanson, David. *War No More: The Case for Abolition*. Charlottesville, VA: David Swanson, 2013.

Thoreau, Henry David. *On the Duty of Civil Disobedience*. Bedford, MA: Applewood, 2000.

Tolstoy, Leo. *War and Peace*. New York: New American Library, 2012.

———. *A Confession and Other Religious Writings*. New York: Penguin, 1987.

Vasconcelos, Jose. *The Cosmic Race/La raza cosmica*. Baltimore: Johns Hopkins University Press, 1997.

Weathers, Glenda B. "Biblical Trees, Biblical Deliverance: Literary Landscapes of Zora Neale Hurston and Toni Morrison." *African American Review* 39:1/2 (2005) 201–12. http://www.jstor.org/stable/40033648.

Westboro Baptist Church. "Open Letter to Lawmakers on Legislation Regarding Her Counter-Demonstrations at Funerals of Dead Soldiers." 2005. http://www.godhatesfags.com/letters/20051212_legislation-message.pdf.

West, Cornel. *The Cornel West Reader*. New York: Basic Civitas, 1999.

———. *Hope on a Tightrope*. New York: SmileyBooks, 2008.

West, Joseph. "Mormon Blood-Atonement." *North American Review* 143:361 (1886) 643–47.

Whitman, Walt. "The 1855 Version of 'Song of Myself.'" In *Walt Whitman's "Song of Myself": A Mosaic of Interpretations*, by Edwin Haveland Miller, 1–44. Iowa City, IA: University of Iowa Press, 1989.

Wyatt, Jean. "Giving Body to the Word: The Maternal Symbolic in Toni Morrison's *Beloved*." In *Critical Essays on Toni Morrison's* Beloved, edited by Barbara H. Solomon, 211–32. New York: G. K. Hall, 1998.

INDEX

abortion, 2–6, 8–11, 24–28, 30–31, 34–41, 44 45, 75 76, 95, 97–98, 101–102
Addams, Jane, 6, 22–23, 47, 54, 55
Alexandre, Sandy, 82
American Civil War, 10, 70, 93
Aristotle, 31
Arner, Rob, 4, 47

Bast, Florian, 87
battle. *See*: war
Beloved, 75–92
Bergthaller, Hannes, 90
Bhagavad Gita, 24
Bible, 63–65, 68–69, 76
blood, 10 18–22, 37, 41–43, 45, 50–53, 72, 80, 87–88, 94–95, 97, 99–100
Book of Mormon, 50
Bushman, Richard, 53
Bushnell, Horace, 94–95, 96
Byrd, Charles Michael, 24

Calvinist, 62–63, 66, 72, 73
Campbell, James, 67
Christ, 1, 12, 42, 47, 49, 52–54, 58, 94, 96–97
Christianity, 4, 7, 46–47, 49, 52, 65, 94, 99
Church of Jesus Christ of Latter Day Saints, The, 50
Citizen Ruth, 35–38
Cobb, Michael, 66
Cold War, 58
COVID-19, 57, 98

Day, Dorothy, 1, 9, 75, 102
DeLillo, Don, 59
Demetrakopoulos, Stephanie, 87
Dietrich, Gabriele, 41–42
Dio, Ronnie James, 68

Eagleton, Terry, 47
Edwards, Jonathan, 64–65
Ehrenreich, Barbara, 26, 46, 75, 99
Emerson, Ralph Waldo, 7, 12, 14–16, 18–19, 74, 99–101
feminism, 31–34, 38
Franklin, Benjamin, 66–67
Friedan, Betty, 33, 35
Fry, Douglas, 97
Furman, Jan, 79, 91

Gellman, Jerome, 84, 85
Girard, Rene, 102
Glaude, Eddie, 78
Goldberg, Bernard, 33
Goss, Chris, 93, 95
Grewal, Gurleen, 79, 85
Grosz, Elizabeth, 24–26, 45
Gustafson, James, 101

Hamner, M. Gail, 56
Hannity and Colmes, 62–63
Hannity, Sean, 62–63, 69
Hauerwas, Stanley, 45, 94, 101
Hedges, Chris, 56
Hinckley, Gordon, 53
Hirschman, Linda, 31–35
Howe, Julia Ward, 70
Hutchinson, Anne, 77

INDEX

James, William, 10–11, 20, 72–73, 96, 99
Juhasz, Susanne, 84

Kant, Immanuel, 14
Kaepernick, Colin, 21, 55
Kierkegaard, Søren, 83–86
King, Rev. Martin Luther King, Jr., 65
Kirkemo, Ronald, 48–49
Kloeckner, Alfred, 19
Kodat, Catherine Gunther, 78
Konstantinov, Vladimir, 58
Kruger, Barbara, 2, 25, 44
Ku Klux Klan, 69, 71

LaBonte, Dennis, 69
Lacan, Jacques, 56

Machiavellian, 49
Madson, Josh, 53
Mandel, Naomi, 89
Manninen, Bertha, 38–39, 44, 45, 76
Masters of Reality, 93
Medoro, Dana, 79, 88
Miller, Perry, 73
Mitchell, Angelyn, 88
Mormon, 51, 53
Morrison, Toni, 43, 76. See: *Beloved*
Mullins, Robert Bruce, 94–95

Nietzsche, Friedrich, 49

O'Reilly, Andrea, 89
Oates, Joyce Carol, 58
Onion, The, 44
Otten, Terry, 81

Paglia, Camille, 39, 40, 42, 97
Paris, Ginette, 5, 88
Phelps, Fred, 62, 69
Plato, 31
pro-choice, 8, 28, 31, 34, 36, 37–38, 40, 45, 75
pro-life, 1, 2, 4–5, 8, 38, 42

rape, 3, 40, 87

Reagan, Leslie, 30
Rodriguez, Eusebio, 78
Roper, Shirley Phelps, 62–63, 69, 71

sacrifice, 2–3, 5–7, 11, 17, 20, 22, 24, 28, 35, 38–39, 42, 45–46, 51–52, 54, 56–57, 59–60, 73, 75–79, 83–85, 91, 93–100, 102
Schadt, Devin, 17
Schneider, Herbert, 67
Scubla, Lucian, 41–42, 75
Singer, Margaret Thaler, 49
soldier, 2, 5, 20, 22–23, 25–26, 48, 54–58, 63, 67, 69–70, 72–73, 97, 99, 101
Star-Spangled Banner, The, 54
Steinem, Gloria, 33
Stout, Harry S., 62, 71, 94
Swanson, David, 97–98
Suckiel, Ellen Kappy, 13

Thoreau, Henry David, 67–68
Tolstoy, Leo, 6, 7, 22–23, 28, 47–48

United States Marine Corps, 50, 56
Utley, Mike, 57–58

Vasconcelos, José, 13
violence, 3–4, 8–9, 15, 18, 20, 27–28, 39–40, 42, 45–47, 49–54, 57–59, 67, 74–76, 78, 82, 96–102

war, 1–6, 8–11, 13, 20, 22–29, 42, 45–49, 53–60, 62, 66–68, 70–75, 94–99, 101–102
warfare. *See*: war
Weathers, Glenda, 82
West, Cornel, 3, 65–66, 68–69, 71, 94
West, Joseph, 51
Westboro Baptist Church (WBC), 62–74, 100
Whitman, Walt, 8
Wright, Jeremiah, 68, 71
World War I, 46, 54
World War II, 1
Wyatt, Jean, 79

www.ingramcontent.com/pod-product-compliance
Lightning Source LLC
Chambersburg PA
CBHW032234080426
42735CB00008B/856